BIBLIOASIS INTERNATIONAL TRANSLATION SERIES

General Editor: Stephen Henighan

Since 2007 the Biblioasis International Translation Series has been publishing exciting literature from Europe, Latin America, Africa and the minority languages of Canada. Committed to the idea that translations must come from the margins of linguistic cultures as well as from the power centres, the Biblioasis International Translation Series is dedicated to publishing world literature in English in Canada. The editors believe that translation is the lifeblood of literature, that a language that is not in touch with other linguistic traditions loses its creative vitality, and that the worldwide spread of English makes literary translation more urgent now than ever before.

1. *I Wrote Stone: The Selected Poetry of Ryszard Kapuściński* (Poland)
   Translated by Diana Kuprel and Marek Kusiba

2. *Good Morning Comrades* by Ondjaki (Angola)
   Translated by Stephen Henighan

3. *Kahn & Engelmann* by Hans Eichner (Austria-Canada)
   Translated by Jean M. Snook

PENSATIVITIES

ESSAYS AND PROVOCATIONS

PENSATIVITIES

ESSAYS AND PROVOCATIONS

MIA COUTO

Translated from the Portuguese
by David Brookshaw

BIBLIOASIS
WINDSOR, ONTARIO

Library and Archives Canada Cataloguing in Publication

Couto, Mia, 1955–
[Essays. Selections. English]
Pensativities : essays / Mia Couto ; translated from the
Portuguese by David Brookshaw.

(Biblioasis international translation series ; no. 14)
Issued in print and electronic formats.
ISBN 978-1-77196-007-6 (paperback).—ISBN 978-1-77196-006-9 (epub)

I. Brookshaw, David, translator   II. Title.   III. Series: Biblioasis
international translation series no. ; 14

PQ9939.C68P46   2015   869.4'5   C2015-902799-3
C2015-902800-0

Selected by Stephen Henighan
Edited by Tara Tobler and Stephen Henighan
Copy-edited by Tara Tobler
Cover design by Kate Hargreaves

These essays are selected from collections originally published as
Pensatempos: Textos de opinião, Editorial Caminho, Lisbon, Portugal, 2005;
E se Obama fosse africano? e outras interinvenções, Editorial Caminho,
Lisbon, 2009; and *Pensageiro frequente*, Editorial Caminho, Lisbon, 2010.

FIRST EDITION.

CONTENTS

FOREWORD

MIA COUTO is Mozambique's best-known writer internationally, and his fiction now appears in more than twenty languages. His first published literary work, in 1983, was as a poet, a genre he has continued to cultivate over the years. His international readership is most familiar with his novels and short stories. Couto is also a highly respected public intellectual, who has written and spoken on a wide range of topical issues relating to African politics and culture. This book is designed to introduce readers of English to a selection of such writings, taken from three collections of essays and autobiographical texts published in Portuguese under the titles of *Pensatempos* (2005), *E se Obama fosse africano? e outras interinvenções* (2009), and *Pensageiro frequente* (2010).

Couto began his writing career as a journalist, serving as director of the Mozambican state news agency, and editor of a daily newspaper and a weekly news magazine in the years immediately following the independence of Mozambique in 1975. He still publishes articles in the press, and his most consistent contributions over the years have taken the shape of the *crónica*: a flexible form whose genre falls somewhere between that of the opinion column, the short story, and the personal anecdote, and whose tradition is highly prized in the Portuguese-speaking press.

The importance of the *crónica* harks back to the emergence of the press in nineteenth century. The genre enabled authors to make social or political comments on topics of popular interest, often using anecdote or the story of a personal experience as their starting point. In this way, serious and sometimes contentious issues could be addressed in a light-hearted, entertaining and often oblique manner, in an environment where democratic institutions and the notion of a free press were still notably fragile. Some of the most widely respected writers of fiction also wrote chronicles for the press in nineteenthth-century Portugal and Brazil. Mia Couto follows in this tradition, and his dedication to what might be considered a hybrid genre is reflected in the fact that some of his chronicles have even been included in his collections of short stories. The world of creative writing and of reportage overlap and often mesh in his work, and this is especially apparent in this collection, in pieces such as "The China within Us," "Land of Water and Rain," and "A Boat in the Sky over Munhava," which contain anecdote, poetic childhood memories, and implied topical comment. They invite us to ponder on the complexities of identity, the contrasts between urban and rural life in a developing country like Mozambique, and the challenges of nature conservation. Indeed, ecological issues are a frequent topic in Mia Couto's essays, as he trained as a biologist, and works in the field of ecological conservation.

In addition to *crónicas*, this collection contains a wide range of Mia Couto's speeches, lectures, and talks. These texts give us his thoughts on African literature and culture, the erroneous views that many in the West have of Africa, and the nefarious effects such views have on the mentalities of emerging elites on the continent. (One such effect includes the spread of what he calls "developmentalese," a linguistic and cultural depenendce on outsiders' prescriptions for development. Couto contends that a younger generation of Africans must overcome this submissiveness to western perceptions, and to do so by finding their own solutions to issues of culture, economics, social opportunity and equality, or natural conservation. Two of the texts also discuss the influence of Brazilian literature on authors of his generation, as Brazilian writers from the mid-twentieth century had adapted the Portuguese language to better reflect their cultural and linguistic diversity. Mozambican writers from the 1960s to the 1980s took that strategy as a model through which to explore African realities. At the same time, a recurring theme in these essays is Couto's rejection of essentialist views of identity, and of so-called African authenticity. For Couto, identity is fluid, prone to change, and above all a narrative, he believes that, Africans should accept their cultural hybridity as a creative force and an expression of their own contribution to modernity.

Readers familiar with Couto's fiction will find material in these essays that complements the themes and ideas suggested in his novels and short stories. Those entering Couto's world through these essays will discover here an essential contribution to contemporary debates about Africa.

— David Brookshaw

THE
FRONTIER OF CULTURE

FOR YEARS, I taught classes in various faculties of the
Eduardo Mondlane University. My teaching colleagues
complained about the progressive decline in the prepa-
ration of students. I noticed something that, for me, was even
more serious: an ever greater remoteness among these young
people from their own country. When they left Maputo to
carry out fieldwork, these youngsters would behave as if they
were emigrating to a strange and hostile universe. They didn't
know the languages, they were ignorant of the cultural codes,
they felt dislocated and yearned for Maputo. Some of them
were haunted by the same spectres as colonial explorers: wild
animals, snakes, invisible monsters.

These rural areas were, after all, the space where their
grandparents and all their ancestors had lived. But they didn't
see themselves as inheritors of this patrimony. Their country
was somewhere else. Worse still: they didn't like this other
nation. And what was still more serious: they were ashamed
of being linked to it. The truth is simple: these young people
are more at ease in front of a Michael Jackson video than in
the garden of a Mozambican country dweller.

What's happening, and this seems inevitable, is that we are creating different citizenships within Mozambique. There are various categories of these: there are the urban citizens, inhabitants of the upper city, those who have been to South Africa more often than they have to the suburbs of Maputo. Then there are those who live on the periphery, the inhabitants of the so-called lower city. And then there are the rural dwellers, those who are a kind of distorted image of the national self-portrait. These people seem doomed to have no face, to speak through the voices of others.

Whether or not the creation of different citizenships (or, more seriously, of different degrees of the same citizenship) is problematic depends on the ability to keep the differing segments of our society in dialogue. The question is: do these different Mozambiques speak to one another?

Our richness derives from our willingness to carry out cultural exchanges with others. President Chissano, in a very recent text, asks what special quality Mozambique possesses, and why it attracts so many visitors. A special *je ne sais quoi* does, indeed, exist. This magic is still alive. But no one thinks, perfectly reasonably, that this power of seduction derives from our being naturally better than others. This magic originates in our ability to exchange culture, to produce hybridities. It originates in our capacity to be ourselves while being others.

I've come here to talk about a very private dialogue, which I very rarely talk about. I am referring to our conversation with our own ghosts. Time has shaped our collective soul by means of three materials: the past, the present, and the future. None of these materials seems to have been made for our immediate use. The past was badly packed and has reached us damaged, loaded with myths and prejudices. The present comes dressed in borrowed clothes. And the future has been commissioned by interests that are alien to us.

I'm not saying anything new: our country isn't poor but it has been impoverished. My argument is that Mozambique's impoverishment doesn't begin with economic explanations. Our greater impoverishment derives from our lack of ideas, from the erosion of our creativity, and from the absence of productive debate. More than impoverished, we have become barren.

I am going to question these three dimensions of time merely by way of provocation. Let us begin with the past, that we may finish by concluding that the past has not yet passed.

What We Were: A Portrait Made by Borrowing

Colonialism didn't die when countries became independent. There was a change of shift and of crew. Present-day colonialism has dispensed with colonials and has become indigenized within our territories. Not only has it been naturalized but it has come to be jointly administered by a partnership between former colonizers and the formerly colonized.

Much of the vision we have of our country's and our continent's past is dictated by the same presuppositions that went into constructing colonial history, or rather, colonized history. A positive sign was placed over what had been negative. The idea persists that pre-colonial Africa was a world beyond time, without conflict or disputes, a paradise made only of harmony.

This romantic image of the past feeds the reductive, simplistic notion of a present condition in which all would be good and function marvellously if it weren't for outside interference. Those to blame for our problems should only be sought outside, and never inside. The few insiders who are bad, are so because they are the agents of outsiders.

This vision was already present in the discourse of the armed struggle, when the enemy were referred to as "infiltrators." This happened in spite of the poet Agostinho Neto's warning, which stated "it is not enough for our cause to be just and pure, but justice and purity must exist within us." Our ranks, in those days, were seen as being composed exclusively of pure folk. If there was a stain, it emanated from outside, the place where the enemy dwelt.

This simplifying, Manichaean approach to "the time that has passed" had another consequence: it perpetuated the idea that sole and exclusive responsibility for slavery and colonialism fell to Europeans.

When the European navigators started to fill their ships with slaves, they weren't the first to traffic in human beings. Slavery had already been invented on all continents. The Americans practised it, as did the Europeans, Asians and even Africans. Slavery was the invention of the human species. What happened was that the slave trade was converted into a global system, and this system was developed in order to enrich its centre: Europe, and later, North America.

I'm going to tell you a curious episode involving an African lady called Honoria Bailor-Caulker, which occurred while she was visiting the United States. Honoria Bailor-Caulker is the mayor of the coastal town of Shenge, in Sierra Leone. It's a small town, but one that's full of history. Thousands of slaves left from there to cross the Atlantic and work in the American sugar plantations.

Honoria was invited to give a speech in the United States. Before a distinguished audience, the lady stepped up to the podium and insisted on exhibiting her vocal resources. To the astonishment of those present, she sang the hymn *Amazing Grace*. At the end, Honoria Bailor-Caulker allowed a heavy silence to descend. In the eyes of the Americans, she seemed to have lost her train of thought. But she began her speech and said: the composer of this hymn was born into the slave system, a descendant of a family from my little town of Shenge.

It was like a stroke of magic, and the audience was split between tears and applause. Those present got to their feet, and possibly out of fellow feeling mixed with a modicum of guilt, they acclaimed Honoria.

"Are you applauding me as a descendant of slaves?" she asked those listening.

The answer was a resounding "yes." That black woman represented, after all, the suffering of millions of slaves to whom America owed so much.

"Well," said Honoria, "in fact I'm not a descendant of slaves. Neither I nor the composer of the hymn. In fact, we are descendants of those who sold slaves. My great-grandparents grew rich selling slaves."

Honoria Bailor-Caulker had the courage to assume, with all honesty, the role opposite to stereotype. But this is such an isolated case that it risks being lost and forgotten.

Colonialism was another disaster, whose human suffering cannot be alleviated. But just as in the case of slavery, colonial domination also had inside help. Various African elites connived in and benefited from this historical phenomenon.

Why am I talking about this? Because I believe that the official History of our continent has been subject to a number of distortions. The first and most heinous was that formulated to justify exploitation for the enrichment of Europe. But other distortions ensued and some of these sought to conceal internal responsibility, to assuage the guilt of certain African social groups that participated from the outset in the oppression of the peoples and nations of Africa. This twisted reading of the past is not merely a theoretical diversion. It ends up giving sustenance to an attitude of eternal victimhood; it suggests false enemies and unprincipled alliances.

It is important that we shine a new light on our past, because what is happening now in our countries is nothing other than a modern recasting of old connivances between interests, internal and external. We are reliving a past that we receive in such a distorted form that we are incapable of recognizing it when it reaches us. We are not far removed from those university students who, when they journey outside of Maputo, do not recognize themselves as the inheritors of the elders.

What We Are: A Mirror in Search of Its Image

If the past reaches us in a state of deformity, so the present flows into our lives, its form incomplete. Some experience this as a drama. And they rush off nervously in search of that which they call our identity. In the vast majority of cases, this identity is a house furnished by ourselves, but the furniture and the house itself were constructed by others. Others believe that the affirmation of their identity stems from denying the identity of others. What's certain is that our affirmation of who we are is rooted in countless misconceptions.

We must affirm that which is ours, some people say. And they are right. At a time when we are all invited to be Americans, such an appeal has every justification.

It therefore makes absolute sense for us to affirm that which is ours. But my question is this: what is truly ours? There are some misunderstandings here. For example: some believe that the *capulana* is a mode of dress that originated here, that is typically Mozambican. On various occasions, I have posed this question to university students: which fruits are ours, as opposed to strawberries, peaches and apples? The answers are once again curious. People believe that the following originated in Africa: cashews, mangoes, guavas, papaya. And so on and so forth. Now, none of these fruits are ours, in the sense that they are native to the continent. Other times, people suggest that we should affirm what is ours by citing the vegetables used in our cuisine. At this point, our Mozambican emblems would include coconut, cassava, sweet potato, and the peanut. All products that were introduced into Mozambique and into Africa. Yet these things end up being ours because, independently of their origins, we have transformed them, refashioned them in our own way. The *capulana* may have originated elsewhere but it is Mozambican in the way that we fasten it. And in the way this cloth now speaks to us. Coconut is Indonesian, cassava is more Latin American than Jennifer Lopez, but the dish we prepare is ours because we have always cooked it our way.

Concepts must be vital implements in our search for our own image. But much of the conceptual framework we use to look at Mozambique is based on catchphrases which, because they have been repeated so often, have ultimately failed to produce any meaning at all. Let me give some examples. We talk a lot about the following:

traditional power structures;
civil society;
rural communities;
subsistence agriculture.

Forgive my offensive incursion into these domains. But I have heartfelt doubts about the operational viability of any of these concepts. I have doubts as to whether these categories suit us and produce real changes.

A Language Called "Developmentalese"

And this is what worries me—rather than encouraging inno-vative, creative thinking, we are working at a superficial level. Mozambican experts and specialists are reproducing the language of others, concerned with the ability to please and cut a good figure in *workshops*. It's an illusion, a game of appearances, for which some of us are well prepared because we know how to speak a language called "Developmentalese." Yet faced with the task of seeking meaningful solutions for national problems, we are as much at a loss as any other ordinary citizen.

Buzzwords such as good governance, accountability, partnerships, sustainable development, building institutional capacity, auditing and monitoring, equity, advocacy, all these fashionable terms give added value (there's another fashionable term) to so-called "panel presentations" (in fact, one should really refer to them as "papers"). But if, when importing these value-added buzzwords, you don't want to be in the same situation as a certain speaker I once saw, you should avoid word-for-word translation—I've already heard someone referred to as a *painelista*, which, apart from being not very nice, is a dangerous word. This speaker, to avoid saying that he was going to give a presentation using PowerPoint, ended up announcing he was going to give a presentation using his "powerful point." This could be susceptible to malicious interpretations.

The problem with Developmentalese is that it only invites one to think what has already been thought by others. We are consumers rather than producers of thought. But it wasn't just a language we created: we created a whole army of specialists, some of them with curious names. I have seen them in a variety of meetings: I've seen specialists in conflict resolution, conference facilitation, workshopping, advocacy, and political engineering.

We are committing our finest human resources to something whose use must be questioned.

The greatest temptation nowadays is for us to reduce issues to their linguistic dimension. We speak, and having spoken, we think we have acted. Often, the same word has danced with a vast number of partners. So many in fact that whatever the party, certain expressions always take to the floor first. One of these words is "poverty." Poverty has already danced with "the decade against underdevelopment," and later with another dancer, calling herself "the struggle against absolute poverty." Also early to the floor are the people, though they specialize in masked balls. The people assumed the mask of "the popular masses." The people have already been "the working masses." After that they were "the population." Now, they dance in the guise of "local communities."

The truth is that we are still hugely ignorant of the current dynamics, the living, practical mechanisms that these so-called people invent in order to survive. We know very little about issues of urgent and primary importance.

It's not only the young students who look at the rural world as if it were an abyss. For us too, there is a Mozambique that remains invisible.

More serious than these omissions is the image that has been created as a substitute for reality. It has become an increasingly common idea that development is the accumulated result of conferences, workshops and projects. And I know of no country that has developed on the basis of projects. You, more than anyone, know this. But whoever reads newspapers realizes how entrenched such beliefs are. All this merely illustrates the appeal of an attitude prevailing among us, which asserts that it is others (in our modern jargon, the "stakeholders") who bear the historic obligation to haul us out of poverty.

Our Being a World: Seeking a Family

At a conference in which I took part this year in Europe, someone asked me: *What is it, for you, to be African?*

And I asked him back: *And what, for you, is it to be European?*

He didn't know what to answer. Similarly, no one knows exactly what is meant by African identity. There's a lot of dross, a lot of folklore, within this spectrum. There are some who say that what is "typically African" is that which carries a greater spiritual weight. I've heard someone say that we Africans are different from others because we give far greater value to our culture. An African specialist at a conference in Prague stated that the measure of Africanness lay in the concept of *ubuntu*, and that this concept states: "I am the others."

Now, all these conjectures seem vague and diffuse to me, all this has surfaced because a questionable history has been accepted as substance. Hasty definitions of African identity rest on a basis of exoticism, as if Africans were unique, or as if their differences were the result of some fact rooted in essence.

Africa cannot be reduced to a facile, easy-to-understand entity. Our continent is made up of profound diversities and complex hybridities. Long and irreversible processes of cultural mingling have moulded a patchwork of differences that constitute one of the most valuable patrimonies of our continent. When we mention these mixtures, we do so with some unease, as if a hybrid product were in some way less pure. But there's no such thing as purity when we talk of the human species. There is no contemporary economy that isn't built on trade. In the same way, there's no human culture that isn't based on far-reaching transactions of the soul.

What We Want and What We Can Be

I'm going to tell you about a true episode, one that occurred near here, in South Africa in 1856. A well-known spirit medium called Mhalakaza claimed that the spirits of his ancestors had transmitted a prophecy to him. It was that a great resurrection would occur and the British would be expelled. For this to happen, the Xhosa people would have to destroy all their livestock and their fields, as a sign of faith and that wealth and abundance would spring from the ground for all. Mhalakaza convinced the rulers of the kingdom of the truth of his vision. Chief Sarili, a member of the Tshawe royal household, proclaimed the prophecy as official doctrine. Quite apart from the soothsayer's vision, Sarili had a strange conviction: it was that the Russians were the ancestors of the Xhosa and would spring from the ground in accordance with the promised resurrection. This idea arose because the Xhosa monarchs had heard talk of the Crimean War and of the fact that the Russians were fighting the British.

The idea spread rapidly that after the Russians had defeated the British in Europe, they would come and expel them from South Africa. And what is even more curious is that it was established that the Russians would be black, under the assumption that all those opposed to British dominion must be black.

I won't linger on the historical episode. The reality is that with the disappearance of their livestock and their agriculture, famine destroyed more than two-thirds of the Xhosa people. One of the greatest tragedies in all African history had been consummated. The drama was exploited by colonial ideology as a proof of extreme superstitiousness on the continent. But the reality is that history is a good deal more complex than simple belief. Behind this whole scenario lurked serious political disputes. Within the Xhosa monarchy, a powerful current of dissidence against this collective suicide took shape. But this group was very quickly labelled "infidels," and a militia made up of "believers" was created in order to repress those who were in disagreement.

It's clear that this story, which is sadly true, cannot be repeated nowadays in the same form. But I'll leave you to consider for yourselves parallels with occurrences in our part of the South, in Africa, in the World. Apprentice witch doctors still construct messianic prophecies and tragically drag whole peoples along with them towards suffering and despair.

Our continent runs the risk of becoming a forgotten territory, of secondary interest to the strategists of global integration. When I say "forgotten," you will think I'm referring to the attitude of the great powers. But I'm referring to our own elites who have turned their backs on their responsibilities towards their own people, to the way their predatory behaviour helps denigrate our image and injures the dignity of all Africans. The discourse of most of our politicians is made up of banalities, incapable of illuminating the complex state of our countries and our peoples. Shallow demagoguery continues to replace the search for solutions. The ease with which dictators take possession of the destinies of entire nations is something that should alarm us. The ease with which present mistakes are explained by blaming the past should worry us all. It's true that corruption and the abuse of power are not, as some would have it, exclusive to our continent. But the space we afford tyrants for manipulation is astonishing. We urgently need to curb the opportunities for the exercise of vanity, arrogance and impunity among those who grow rich through robbery. We urgently need to redefine the premises upon which our management models are predicated, and which exclude those who live outside the sphere of literacy and on the periphery of European logic and rationality.

We Mozambicans are living through a very particular moment of our history, with some perplexity. Until this point, Mozambique believed it could dispense with a radical interpretation of its very foundations. The Mozambican nation gained an epic sense of itself in its struggle against external forces. Hell was always elsewhere, the enemy was beyond its borders. It was Ian Smith, apartheid, imperialism. In the end, the country did what we all do in our everyday lives: we invent monsters in order to unsettle ourselves. But monsters also serve to placate us. We feel at ease knowing that they dwell outside us. Suddenly, the world has changed and we are forced to seek our demons within our own home. The enemy, the worst of our enemies, was always within us. We have discovered this simple truth and we are left alone with our own ghosts. And that has never happened to us before.

This is a moment of bleakness and despair. But it may also be a moment of growth. Confronted with our most deeply felt vulnerabilities, we must create a new vision, invent other utterances, attempt different scriptures. We are ever more alone in our historic responsibility to create another History. We cannot beg the world for another image. We cannot persist in an attitude of appeal. The only solution is to continue the long, hard journey towards conquering a place of which we and our nation are worthy. And that place can only be the product of our own creation.

Talk given to the Association of
Mozambican Economists, Maputo, August, 2003.

OUR
POOR RICH PEOPLE

T HE GREATEST misfortune for a poor country is that, instead of producing wealth, it produces rich people. But rich people without wealth. In fact, it would be better to call them moneyed rather than rich: a rich person is one who possesses the means of production. A rich person is someone who generates money and provides jobs. A moneyed person is someone who quite simply has some cash. Or rather, he thinks he has. For, in reality, it's the cash that has him.

The truth is this: our rich are too poor. What they have, they don't hold on to. Worse still, that which they exhibit as being theirs is the property of others. It's the product of robbery and sharp practice. Yet, our moneyed friends are unable to enjoy all they have stolen in peace and quiet. They live obsessed by the possibility that they may be robbed. They would need a police force of an appropriate standard. But a police force of an appropriate standard would throw them all in jail. They would need a social order in which there were few reasons to pursue crime. But if they have grown rich, it is precisely thanks to this same disorder.

The biggest dream of our new-rich in the end is quite small: a luxury car, a bit of temporary bling. But the luxury car cannot have too many dreams of its own, as it is shaken by the potholes of the city thoroughfares. A Mercedes or a BMW can't make full use of its lustre, as it busily swerves to avoid the very convex buses along very concave roads. The existence of good roads would depend upon another type of wealth. A wealth that might serve the city. And the wealth of our new-rich originated in an opposing trend: the impoverishment of our city and our society.

The luxury houses of our false rich are designed less for living and more for being seen. They were built for the eyes of those passing by. But as they exhibit themselves in this way, full of frills and showing off, they end up attracting the greed of outsiders. No matter how many guards they may have at the door, our poor-rich cannot escape the fear of envy and the spells and curses that this envy invites. The solemn grandeur of their residences doesn't make them immune. Our poor little rich people!

They are like a glass of draft beer. They are poured in an instant, but they're mostly froth. Anything real that's left belongs to the glass rather than the content. They could raise livestock or grow vegetables. But no. Instead, our moneyed friends, poured out on tap, create lovers. But these lovers (whether female or male) are a source of serious inconvenience: they need to be maintained with expensive gifts. The biggest snag, however, is the absence of any product guarantee. Someone's lover today may be another's tomorrow. The collector of lovers finds no peace of mind: whoever has betrayed, may be betrayed.

Our hurriedly assembled moneyed classes don't feel comfortable in their own skins. They dream of being Americans, South Africans. They aspire to be others, far removed from their origins, their condition. And so there they are imitating others, assimilating the foibles of the really rich, from places that are really rich. But our aspiring entrepreneurs aren't even capable of resolving the most basic dilemma: why they can buy appearances, but they cannot buy the respect and affection of others. Those others who see them parading their barely explained luxuries. Those others who recognize within them the translation of a lie. Our moneyed elite isn't an elite: it's a distortion, a hasty imitation.

The struggle for national liberation was guided by a moral principle: it was not intended to substitute an exploiting elite with another one, even if it was of a different racial composition. They didn't want a mere change of shift among oppressors. Today, we are on the threshold of a decision: who are we going to play in the race for development? Is it these people who are going to represent us on the field known as "the struggle for progress"? Our new-rich (who can't even explain where their money came from) have already picked themselves for the squad, anxious to take their turn in pillaging the country. They are national representatives, but only in appearance. For they're prepared to be the servants of others, of foreigners. As long as these others promise them reward enough, they'll end up selling off the little we have left.

Some of our moneyed elites are not far removed from the kids who ask to look after our cars. Our aspirants for power ask to look after the country. The donating community can go shopping or go and have a relaxed lunch, safe in the knowledge that the elite will look after the nation.

Our moneyed elite reflect a childish image of who we are. They're like children who go into a candy store. They go weak-kneed, fascinated by the array of ostentatious goods. They help themselves to the public purse as if it were their own personal pot of money. Their arrogance shames us, as does their lack of culture, their scorn for the people, their elitist attitude towards poverty.

How I wish Mozambique had rich people with a true, honestly earned wealth! Rich people who loved and defended their country and its people. Rich people who created wealth. Who provided jobs and developed the economy. Who obeyed the rules of the game. In short, rich people who enriched us.

Let's hope our elite commits suicide alone. Don't let them drag us and the whole country into the abyss.

Published in the Mozambican newspaper,
Savana, December, 2002

A WORD OF ADVICE
AND SOME ADVICE
WITHOUT WORDS

I AM A WRITER and a scientist. I see the two activities, writing and science, as being close and complementary. Science lives on our inquisitiveness, on our desire for boundless knowledge. Writing is a false tranquillity, a capacity to feel boundless. Both result from the refusal to accept frontiers, both are a desired step beyond the horizon. Biology, for me, isn't just a scientific discipline, but a story to enchant us, the story of the oldest journey, which is that of Life. This is what I ask of science: that it may induce in me a passion. That's precisely what I ask of literature.

Young people often ask me how one writes a literary text. The question is not without justification. But what should be questioned is how one maintains a relationship with the world through writing literature. How does one feel in such a way that others feel represented by us through a story? In truth, writing is not a mechanical exercise, and one doesn't construct a poem or a short story in the same way that one carries out an operation in arithmetic. Writing always demands poetry. And poetry is another way of thinking that lies beyond the logic taught to us by school and the modern world. It's another window that opens so that we can begin to look differently at objects and creatures. Without the arrogance of trying to understand them. Merely with an illusory attempt to enter into kinship with the world.

There are no ready-made formulas for imagining and writing a short story. My secret (and it only works for me) is to allow myself to be enchanted by stories I listen to, by characters I meet, and to leave myself open to the tiny details of everyday life. The writer's secret is prior to the act of writing. It's in life, in the way he makes himself available and allows himself to absorb the minor details of daily life.

A short story is made up of brush strokes. It's a picture without a frame, the unfinished beginning of a story that has no end. A short story doesn't cover whole lifespans. It shines a brief light on lives. One instant, one flash of light. The important thing is not what it reveals, but what it suggests, stimulating the reader's complicit curiosity. In a short story, the important element isn't so much the plot but the ability to catch the human soul in the act. In a short story (as in any literary genre), the most important thing is not its literary content but the way it moves us and teaches us to understand, not through our power of reasoning but through our emotion (can it be that these two categories are so separate?).

In science (as in other activities), the most important thing is not that which we call scientific. It's the human aspect. The idea sprang up that the scientist is exempt from error: a kind of privileged being who only treads the paths of rigour and precision. This idea suggests that error is the enemy of science. The aversion to error is, in itself, the gravest of errors. It is as vital for us to get things wrong as it is to get things right. We should maintain our taste for experimentation, even if we make mistakes. Nature evolved gradually thanks to a basic error, which is mutation. If genes never failed, then life wouldn't have the diversity necessary to continue. Vital processes demand rigour and error at the same time. We mustn't be afraid of not knowing. What we should fear is not being inquisitive enough to arrive at knowledge.

My friend Quintanilha will be able to tell you about the discovery of the first antibiotic by Alexander Fleming. This scientist didn't have an exact idea of what was happening when he noticed a strange stain developing on the petri dishes in his laboratory. It was almost by accident that he discovered penicillin, a medication that would save millions of human lives. The Watson-Crick duo resolved the issue of the three-dimensional architecture of DNA, not just by studying its structure but because they allowed themselves to be assailed by intuitions of an aesthetic kind. The German poet, Goethe, carried out important discoveries in the morphology of plants by coupling his poetic intuition with empirical observation.

People ask me how I deal with scientific subjects in a short story. Some of you have sent me stories that focus on the challenge of research. A short story isn't driven by a great scientific discovery, or by scientific fact itself. What drives a short story is the internal conflict within people, or the tiny detail of a person who surprises him or herself, and discovers someone else. What a short story can evoke is the degree to which, within every scientist, there is a man: a man complete with ignorance, uncertainties, and beliefs that often have little to do with science. Let us imagine, for example, that we are privy to the day-to-day life of an astronomer who spends his life peering into the darkness of the Universe, looking for black holes. And we discover that, during the night, he has to sleep with the light on, and only falls asleep when holding his wife's hand, because he's scared of the darkness in his room. This could be the motif for a beautiful story. Deep down, even the most modern and renowned scientist still has to confront our most timeless obsessions. Science is an answer. Not the answer. We shall always have to face our most ancient fears.

So the only advice I have is this: listen. Become more attentive to the voices that we have been encouraged to no longer hear. Let us become these voices made visible. And let us keep alive that ability we had when children to be dazzled. By simple things, that can be found in the margins of great deeds. A school handyman, an assistant who provides support in laboratory classes, can be more persuasive than the most prestigious academic. What is important from the point of view of a writer is the capacity such a character may have to evoke stories and reveal to us facets of our own humanity.

The country where I was born and where I live—Mozambique—is a poor country and only a tiny few have access to what we call science. But in the rural areas, there are people who, though illiterate, are knowledgeable. I learn a lot from these men and women who are able to resolve problems using a type of logic that my brain was never taught. This rural world, far from scientific manuals, possesses no less knowledge than the urban world we inhabit. Our willingness to listen while on this borderline can be a deep source of pleasure. One can only tell a beautiful story by taking delight in the enterprise.

I come back, at last, to the world of literary writing. One only writes with any intensity by living intensely. It's not just a question of living one's feelings but of being lived by feelings. School very often advises us to look at the world through one window, and to believe all truth has the imprimatur of science. And so we stifle our willingness to see other truths. We become all the poorer, more concentrated on our isolation.

There are those who believe that science is an instrument enabling us to rule the world. But I would rather see scientific knowledge as a means, not to dominate, but to find harmony. To create as a means of expression through which we may share with others, including those beings we believe to have no means of expression. To understand and share the language of trees, the silent discourse of stones and stars.

To gain knowledge not in order to claim ownership. But to gain the companionship of the living and non-living creatures we share this world with. To listen to stories that are told to us, at any hour of the day, by these creatures.

Text elaborated for the children of the Lusophone countries,
participating in the Living Science
Program, Portugal, July, 2004.

WHAT AFRICA DOES THE AFRICAN WRITER WRITE ABOUT?

THE THEME of this event is the writer's relationship with the struggle for a world that is more humane and more democratic. One could begin with this question: what is the writer's responsibility towards democracy and human rights? It is total. For the writer's greatest commitment is with truth and freedom. To fight the cause of truth, the writer uses an untruth: literature. But it is a lie that doesn't lie.

However, the writer has other commitments. One of the duties of an African writer is to be willing, in certain circumstances, to stop being a writer, and to not think of himself as "African."

Let me explain: the writer is someone who should be open to travelling through other experiences, other cultures, other lives. He should be willing to deny his own self. For only by doing this will he journey between identities. And that is what a writer is—a traveller between identities, a smuggler of souls. There isn't a writer who doesn't share this condition: of being a creature of the frontier, someone who lives by a window, the window that looks out over interiorized territories.

Our role is to create the guiding principles for a line of thinking that belongs more to us, so that the assessment of our place and our time may cease to be made on the basis of categories created by others, and so that we may go on to tackle that which seems to us to be most natural and beyond question: concepts of human rights, democracy, Africanness. It is precisely our relationship with Africa that I would like to question here. Why this "Africanness," raised to the level of identity, has been the object of continual mystification.

Some people hurriedly seek an essential quality for what they call "Africanness." On the surface, they are busy seeking the roots of their pride in being African. But, in the end, they show a similarity to colonial ideology. Africa cannot be reduced to a simple entity, easy to understand and fit into the compendia of Africanists. Our continent is the result of diversities and hybridities.

When we talk of hybridities, we have to be careful, as a hybrid product can seem somehow less "pure." But there's no such thing as purity when one is talking of the human species. And if we enter into hybrid relationships, it means that someone else, on the other side, has received something that was ours.

The defenders of African purity redouble their efforts to find its essence. Some set off to prospect in the deep past. Others seek to situate African authenticity in the rural tradition, as if the modernity that Africans are inventing in the urban areas weren't itself similarly African. This restricted and restrictive vision of what is genuine may well be one of the main reasons why literature in Africa is viewed with suspicion. Literature goes hand in hand with modernity. And we lose our "identity" if we cross the frontier out of traditionalism: that's what the preconceived notions the hunters of ethnic and racial virginity tell us.

The opposition between the traditional—seen as the pure, uncontaminated side of African culture—and the modern is a false contradiction, for the rural cosmovision is equally the product of exchanges between different cultural worlds. The vast majority of young people from the rural culture of my country dream of being Michael Jackson or Eddie Murphy. In a word, they dream of being black Americans.

"Here I am," wrote Léopold Senghor, "trying to forget Europe in the heart of Senegal." The Senegalese poet and statesman never managed it. He was himself a bridge between two continents. Nor could he have been otherwise. To forget Europe cannot be to eliminate the internal conflicts that have shaped our very identities. Europe was inside the African poet and it could not be forgotten by imposition.

Between the invitation to forget Europe and the dream of being American, the outcome can only be seen as a step forward. African intellectuals shouldn't be ashamed of their predilection for hybridity. They don't need to fit the image of European myths concerning them. They don't need artifices or fetishes in order to be African. They are Africans just as they are, urban dwellers with a mixed and tangled-up soul, because Africa has every right to modernity, it has every right to assume its hybridities, which it initiated itself and which make it more diverse and therefore richer.

We need to escape from this trap, and that can only be done by those Africans prepared to accept, without fear, their membership in a culturally mixed world. Some self-styled Africanists, no matter how much they may resist so-called European concepts, nevertheless remain prisoners of these same concepts. Nor is it that they attach importance to them, but rather that importance is accorded for negative reasons. It's not a question of finding identity by retreating into ancestral purity. The most ferocious defenders of African cultural nationalism are designing houses that are contrary to, but still within the overall framework of the architecture of the Other, of that which we call Western. A fetishistic attitude, however, turned towards customs, folklore, tradition, is of little

value. Colonial domination invented a considerable proportion of Africa's past and tradition.

In fact, the obsession with classifying what is and is not
"African" began in Europe. Ethnography and anthropology,
disciplines that, until recently, sought to identify essence
rather than process, also trod that path. The discoverers of
identities were like navigators of the sixteenth century: anxious, some of them, to baptize territories that had long been
baptized; others, in a hurry to label population groups
whose characteristics they didn't even know (tribes, ethnic
groups, clans).

Think, for instance, of the culture produced by Africans.
Instead of valuing the diversity of such production and seeing the book as a cultural product, literary appreciation is
often replaced by a more or less ethnographic set of values. The question posed is the extent to which the author is
"authentically African." No one knows exactly what it is to be
"authentically African." But the book and its author still need
to undergo this test of identity. Or a certain idea of identity.

Demands are made of an African writer that are not made
of a European or American writer. Insistence is made on
proof of authenticity. Questions are asked about the degree
to which he is ethnically genuine. No one questions whether
José Saramago represents Portuguese culture. It's irrelevant
to know whether James Joyce corresponds to the cultural
standards of this or that European ethnic group. Why should
African writers have to show such cultural passports? This
happens because people persist in thinking of the production of these African writers as belonging to the domain of
anthropology or ethnography. What they are producing isn't
literature but a transgression against what is accepted as tra-
ditionally African.

The writer isn't just someone who writes. He's someone who produces thought, someone capable of pollinating
others with feeling and delight.

More than this, the writer challenges the basis of thought itself. He goes further than challenging the limits of political correctness. He subverts the very criteria that define what is correct, he questions the boundaries of reason.

Mozambican writers nowadays fulfill a commitment of an ethical type: to reflect on this Mozambique but to dream of another Mozambique. They run the risk, like all artists in every other country, of being devoured by the nation they helped to liberate.

We have passed from a period in which our heroes always ended up dead—Eduardo Mondlane, Samora Machel, Carlos Cardoso—into a time when heroes are not even born. We await the renewal of a state of passion that we experienced once before, while hoping for the rekindling of love between writing and the nation as a home made for dreaming. We want and dream of a nation and a continent that no longer need heroes.

Address given at the award ceremony for the
International Prize for the Twelve Best African Novels,
Cape Town, South Africa, July 2002.

THE FLY
OR THE SPIDER?

W HAT can a writer say on a theme such as the one
proposed: "The Globalization of Computer
Technology"? A number of things occurred to me
as I thought about the subject. I was preparing this address
in the silence of an old room, when I happened to see a spider's web in a corner of the ceiling. This little creature hadn't
planned and built a house to live in, but a trap to hunt its prey.
The English call this weaving together of threads a web. A web
can mean a network, but it can also be a trap. This ambiguity
triggered an old concern of mine. I would like to share my
disquiet with you.

I am worried by the way we are being tempted to view
technology as the global antidote to our multiple evils. Many
of us believe that technological advance is going to rescue us
from poverty. This belief leaves us vulnerable to a few sellers
of magical products. The future may not just be better—as the
slogan tells us—but easier, as easy as pressing a key. For us to
be like them, the developed world, it will be enough for us to
fulfill certain indicators within the criteria presented by our
advisers, and hey presto, we'll join the club.

We know this isn't true. I don't know why we want so much to be like "them," and not ourselves, following our own routes to destinations that we have invented on our own. What separates us from wealth involves, above all, questions of nature rather than technology. It involves attitudes, wishes, political determination and a stance with respect to the question of culture. Digitalization won't convert us into modern beings. Putting our ear to a cellphone isn't going to turn us into producers of anything at all. If we don't exercise any independence in acts that are, at heart, acts of culture, we shall enter the universe of what we call the digital society, but we shall do it as a minor player, a secondary partner, from the periphery.

But this is a dance one joins without warning and without invitation. We're already there, dazzled by the lights and the sound of the orchestra. But we're not dancing to our own music, nor are we swaying to a rhythm that belongs to the body of our History.

We have all entered the dance hall: if we were supposed to pay for a ticket, then someone else has paid for us. Tomorrow, we'll have to pay off the debt with interest. And we shall discover the bitter taste of a hangover (or, as we call it here, a *babalaze*).

I don't intend to make excuses for anything. After all, it's inevitable that we should embrace the lustre of all these digital innovations. But I would just like to be sure that we are thinking about our place in this world, we who are a nation profoundly influenced by orality. And that we are working out how we may stand to gain if we develop our own project, capable of introducing changes and innovations into the projects of others. I would like to know whether we are sufficiently aware of how much we shall lose from this network of relationships to which we belong in the public space of our everyday lives. Rumours about unofficial markets, gossip concerning unofficial bus services: aren't these the invaluable web pages of the Mozambican Internet?

I'm not an advocate of traditionalist solutions, but I worry about the easy availability of magic wands, fantastic solutions that we arrive at as if they were downloaded. Technical and scientific discoveries are presented to us in a messianic way in the pages of magazines: the genome is a new Christ able to save us from all illnesses, cloning is a passport to eternity. The idea hasn't changed since the green revolution was first heralded in the 1970s as a way to salvage agriculture in poor countries. The green revolution has faded in colour, but other magical packages in countless other hues are still being exported to the Third World.

Until a few years ago, the frontier between the civilized and indigenous was to be abolished by the latter's integration into European culture. Now, a new frontier may be emerging: on the one hand are the digitalized, and on the other, the ex-indigenous, destined to become the indigent and indigitalized. A new plan for citizenship is being drawn up. And, once again, we shall dwell on the periphery.

And so the Web is a network but also a spiderweb; this web that we have joined of our own accord, we shall be the spider as long as we develop a strategy. We shall be the fly if we persist in thinking with the mind of others.

An Episode Evoked

I am going to tell you an episode that really happened, and which may illustrate what I have been talking about. We were in the middle of the floods, the great inundations of the year 2000, when we were discovered by the international television channels (it's incredible how only disaster turns the poor into a story). At that point, the Polana Hotel suddenly became a global telecommunications hub, an operational base for the BBC, CNN and other stations vying with each other over the tragedy. I'm not saying this was a bad thing. If it wasn't for this intervention, then the drama of the floods wouldn't have gained any visibility, and we would have received far less support. These latest floods were, in fact, an example of how the negative tendency of scratching around for disasters can sometimes work in our favour, to benefit those who are the eternal victims.

During those days, we were the centre of the universe. Many people in this world, which aspires to be a global village, were seeing the name and face of Mozambique for the first time. It wasn't just Rosita who was born in unusual circumstances (in the canopy of a tree). For a large swathe of global television viewers, the image of ourselves as a country was being born.

We were in the middle of all this uproar when I got a nerve-wracking telephone call from London requesting a live television interview. Worse still, it would have to be in English. I was nervous. To speak live on the BBC and in English is to be catapulted into a terrain that is doubly unfamiliar and foreign.

We arranged for it to be at 10:30 at night and for me to go to the Polana Hotel. On the agreed night, I arrived and they told me to get into a "chapa" (which, as you know, is an unofficial vehicle for transporting passengers), and along with a team of journalists I set off on a nightmarish journey through the suburbs of Maputo. The journalists were all kitted out in uniform—khaki suits that were part military, part neo-ecological. I don't know whether journalists assigned to work in the tropics always invest in this mythical attire. But those accompanying me in the old chapa had assumed the posture and the behaviour of newminted and semi-debonair Rambos, garbed at a branch of the Safari Store.

I'd already seen this when I was a journalist myself. The journalist credits himself with a mission, and this mission bears a remarkable similarity to a military operation: there is a need to conquer an audience, and bombard it with news in a premium timespan that is calculated down to the very second. The journalist is on top of what is happening as if the event were a precise target. The event is the prey of that spider who is the reporter, in this web of news that envelops the planet.

We drove for about half an hour and when we stopped, I found myself in the middle of the Polana Caniço area, on the edge of a huge hole. It was the biggest hole I'd ever seen—not that I'm a specialist in holes, but Mozambicans have a credible level of expertise when it comes to cratered roads.

The side of a hill in the so-called Maputo "barreiras," or cliffs, had collapsed during the cyclone, opening up a crater of some fifteen metres in depth and wider than the eye could see. I later learned that more than 27,000 cubic metres of sand had been lost as a result of the hillside's collapse. I was therefore on the edge of an abyss, as if the earth had been swallowed up by the earth itself. My fear was indescribable: I'd just published *The Last Flight of the Flamingo* and, in that story, an entire country disappeared, swallowed up by the earth. Just like one of the book's characters, I was on the brink of an abyss that devoured entire nations.

On the edge of the crater, as if under the volcano of so-called "news," the technicians from the BBC had set up an even more surrealist scene. They had closed off an area of some thirty square metres with a yellow tape on which were written the words "NO ENTRY." In the middle of the darkness, they had opened up an illuminated space like a stage bathed in an intense light, in a world in which only that which can be turned into a spectacle is visible.

On one side, there was a whole panoply of machines, generators, flashlights, transmission hubs, satellite phones, hundreds of cables and wires. It was like a football stadium, with the floodlights directed at an empty centre. Around this floodlit terrain, hundreds of spectators drawn there by curiosity were seated, in a state of animated excitement. Suddenly, an area where nothing ever happened seemed to have become the centre of the technological world.

As I drew near and advanced through the crowd, I noticed there was a discussion taking place. Different opinions jostled with one another:

"Is this a cinema, are they making a film?"

"No," others said, "it's an operation to fill the hole."

"Wow! The government's doing a good job, the hole was only opened up yesterday, and the engineers are already here with their machines."

When I crossed the yellow tape, it was as if I suddenly became someone from another world. All eyes were focussed on me, and a deep silence descended. I had breached the forbidden line and penetrated an illuminated world. Suddenly, a youngster jumped up and pointed to me, shouting:

"Hey, folks! Didn't I say this was a cinema? That guy over there is Chuck Norris!"

This gave rise to an immediate lively ruckus. Chuck Norris—a kind of 007 for the underdeveloped world—was right there in the middle of Polana Caniço? At first, some remained skeptical. But then, there was general clamour. And the crowd shouted at me, waving their arms, showing me their children. Some more daring youngsters weaved vigorous karate blows, freeing themselves from invisible enemies, showing me that my martial art skills didn't just figure on the cinema screen.

The interview was about to begin and technicians were attaching wires, microphones and earphones to me, when the program's producer realized it would be impossible to record anything in the middle of such an uproar. In a panic, they asked me to address the crowd and ask them to be quiet. I walked over to the people and asked them not to make a noise. Their reaction was immediate:

"Wow! The fellow speaks Portuguese! Hey, Chuck Norris pal, ask those guys to fill in this hole!"

Then, there was a flood of requests. The road needed repair-
ing, they needed a health centre, a school, houses. I should put
an end to all the robberies round here, I could do that in the
twinkling of an eye. Everything needed to be done urgently.
I couldn't undo the illusion. I left any explanations for later.
For the time being, we urgently needed silence. And this was
obtained thanks to a surprising misunderstanding that conferred upon Norris a level of respect not shown to mere mortals.
I went back into the circle of light and they loaded me down out
again with all the technology. Once again, there were the wires,
the earphone, the lights, the camera test. We were already connected to London and I was having a preparatory chat with the
interviewer when, in the middle of the crowd, a young man
with a bottle of beer in his hand, got up and shouted:

"Hey, brothers! That guy there isn't Chuck Norris. I know
that dude: it's Mia Couto."

In an instant, the chaos resumed. Everyone debated my
true identity at the tops of their voices. Yet again, the British
freed me from my wires and begged me to ask for silence.
Over to the edge of the lit area I went, and like a preacher,
uttered my appeal. But it was an almost impossible mission.
Someone asked me:

"Mia Couto, why were you pretending to be Chuck
Norris?"

At this point, a tall boy carrying a backpack, emerged
from the mass of human beings and waving some sheets of
paper, challenged me:

"Mister Writer, do you want me to make sure everyone's
quiet? Leave it to me. But you'll owe me a favour afterwards."

There was nothing else for it but to accept. But I needed
to know what I was agreeing to. When I asked him, the young
fellow explained:

"The favour I want is for you to correct this book I've
written."

Our agreement was signed and sealed immediately. The lad must have had some influence over all the others because everyone stopped talking when he waved his arms. Then, he stepped forward with great care so as not to tread on anyone and handed me a sheaf of handwritten papers. On the cover was written: *The Panel Beater's Manual*!

I tucked the papers under my arm and went back to the spot where I was going to be interviewed. The journalists were in a state of panic, and there was no time for rehearsals, instructions, preliminaries, anything. It was a question of hitching me up to the wires and starting. It must have been the worst interview I'd given in my life. Surrounded by a cloud of crickets that had been attracted by the lights, hugging the future *Panel Beater's Manual*, and still glimpsing one or two youngsters waving to me or practising kung-fu, I wasn't even aware of whether I was really speaking English.

Today, as I recall this episode, I think about that place, in the middle of the suburban shanties, about that frontier between light and darkness, and how it symbolized the dividing line between two worlds—the real world and that other, digitalized world. And there I was hopping across this dividing line like a smuggler. But only I and one or two Mozambican technicians were able to cross it. The others were prisoners within this frame of invisibility and silence. The same lights that illuminated me within that virtual space, cast the surrounding world into darkness, obscuring that place where the deep heart of Mozambique pulsates.

Lecture to the Conference of the Mozambican
Telecommunications Company (TDM) on the Globalization
of Technology in a Computerized World, Maputo, April, 2001.

CITIZENSHIP IN SEARCH OF ITS CITY

Defining the Terms

T HE THEME of this seminar is "The Construction of Citizenship in Mozambique." It's important for us to begin by sketching out a set of generally agreed markers and by initiating dialogues based on the same definitions, with a common understanding of words and concepts.

Words and concepts are alive, they wriggle away from us like fish between the hands of thought. And like fish, they swim the length of the river of History. There are those who think they can fish for and freeze concepts. Such people are, at the very least, collectors of dead ideas.

The Mobility of our Identity

The example I want to bring to your attention here is a reworking of that admirable book by Amin Maalouf, entitled *In the Name of Identity: Violence and the Need to Belong*. I experienced an episode which is very close to the one recounted in that excellent work. During the 1980s, I was a journalist.

Let us imagine the following possible scenario: at that time, I might have met a journalist who, upon introducing himself, proudly proclaimed, "I am Yugoslavian." The journalist (who is mirrored almost exactly in Maalouf's essay) was on the board of directors of the newspaper of the party in power. Later, during the same conversation, he let it be understood that he was Islamic in origin, born in the Federated Republic of Bosnia-Herzegovina.

We kept in touch and, during the nineties, at the height of the war in the Balkans, the same man told me with the same fervour: "Don't forget that, before anything else, I'm a Muslim." Later, a mutual friend of ours, working in Mozambique, showed me a photo of the journalist. He was unrecognizable, with a bushy beard that covered his whole face. On the back was written: "Here is the portrait of a true Bosnian."

In fact, I ran into the journalist this year in Paris. He lives as an immigrant in France. And he confessed to me as I left him: "Today I know that, above all else, I'm a European."

We could ask: when did this journalist truly identify himself? Probably always. His identity was drawn and redrawn by his own life experiences. That man never ceased to be waylaid by History.

We, in Mozambique, have not undergone such dramatic changes. But History has occasionally ambushed us as well. Those who, like me, are forty or fifty years old have already lived through very different historical realities. They have belonged to many Mozambiques. At first, they belonged to colonial Mozambique. To a Mozambique that wasn't yet Mozambique. At that time, they spent their money in a bar belonging to a Portuguese who, sometimes, got the local language right but always gave them back the wrong change. They didn't spend much because money was scarce. Then came Independence, and the bar owner packed up his life in a hurriedly filled barrel. The bar owner left the country and Mozambique embarked on socialism. So now we spent our money in the

People's Store. (Spent is a euphemism, because there was nothing to spend our money on.) Then came what, for want of a better term, we call the civil war and the ex-bar became the ex-People's Store. Everything went up in flames and even the bar owner's nostalgia was burnt up in some far corner of Portugal. Finally, capitalist Mozambique arrived and the bar reopened with an owner who occasionally gets the language right, but still gives us the wrong change.

But it wasn't only the country that underwent change. We changed. Our own notion of who we are was modified. During the seventies and eighties, our identity was straight-forward and homogeneous: we were Mozambicans. And that was it. It was unthinkable, at that moment in time, to conceive of ourselves as Makua, Makonde, black, mulatto, white.

Generally speaking, the main feature of our identity, as far as we are all concerned, is still the fact of being Mozambican. But nowadays, other forms of belonging are beginning to take shape. For many of us, other primary forms of iden-tity are emerging. They may be racial, or tribal, or religious identities. This sense of belonging may collide with what we call "Mozambicanness." To think that I may ally myself with someone because we are of the same race isn't just mistaken but it is historically unproductive.

Today some of the possible questions may be: am I a white Mozambican or a Mozambican white? Am I an Indian African or an African Indian? Am I a Muslim Mozambican or vice versa? These terms may look the same but they aren't always so. We may be different things. The mistake is made when we only want to be one thing. The mistake is made when we want to deny that we are various things at the same time. As Simone de Beauvoir would have said: *We aren't born white or black, we sometimes become white or black.*

I'm going to tell you a true story. The managers of my company are Muslims. Quite by chance, I happened to be sit-ting at the desk of one of them when the phone rang. It was a new client who thought he was speaking to a colleague of mine called Amade, and he immediately introduced himself in the following way:

"Assalaam aleikum, bey?"

Then, in the face of my reticence, he realized that the person at the end of the line wasn't the person he thought it was. It was someone else. With some hesitation, he asked to speak to Sr. Amade. At that point, my colleague appeared, they both spoke, and quickly reached an understanding.

It wasn't about any particular request, any unmentionable favour. But the man clearly felt more at ease speaking with his brother in religion. This may reveal complicities that should be avoided, but in itself, it is not a mortal sin. A woman often feels more at ease talking to another woman. And there's no attitude of exclusion in this case.

What happens is that we have created a system that causes difficulties, even over the most trivial matters. Difficulty creates an opportunity for gaining advantage, for various types of opportunism. This system isn't exclusive to Mozambique. It is common throughout the world. But this system makes us feel alienated, insignificant and dislocated. It's the policeman, the teacher, the nurse, the tax man, the official, it's a whole conspiracy of people who earn their living by complicating our lives. In this sea of complicating factors, it's good to hear someone at the other end of the phone line whom we recognize as being one of "ours," someone from our region, our ethnic group, our sex, our religion.

On the surface, it's not wrong for someone to make use of one of their multiple identities to navigate these murky waters. What certainly is wrong is to attempt to create hierarchies: those who are more Mozambican, those who are less Mozambican. What can be dangerous is to create "fortress identities," identities born from negating the identities of others.

The truth is that no one is "pure." This human species of ours is made from mixtures. We've been crossing, exchanging genes, trading values for millions of years. We've been able to survive because of this diversity. There's no one in this room who doesn't have a multifaceted, plural identity. Identities, my friends, are like the fingers of a hand. From time to time, one of these fingers swells up and conceals the other fingers. Each one of us, at a certain point in our lives, has felt this swelling in our soul. There were days when we belonged to more than one ethnic group, one religion, one club. But our hand is still composed of multiple fingers.

On one occasion, someone asked a famous American musician, Ben Harper, this question:

"We've heard you now have a new drummer in your band. Tell me something: is he black?"

And Harper replied:

"I don't know, I've never asked him."

The Taste for Debate

Many of the debates that cut across our public space nowadays are strange. Sometimes, they descend into aggression. We stop discussing ideas in order to attack people. The need to be right, to win at all costs, destroys our civic duty, which is one of our reasons for being here. Debates should be used to arrive collectively at productive concepts, to create ideas that may help build a better Mozambique. We already have to contend with too many destructive and divisive factors.

Just recently, for example, an Internet forum was created to debate the nationality of Eusébio. Young folk ask whether Eusébio is Mozambican or not, to what extent he should feel or can possibly be Portuguese, whether he can be Portuguese and Mozambican.

We have to be careful. We should be wary of the ease with which we invade the souls of others. Who can authorize us to talk so lightly about other people? No citizenship can give me the right to speak in public about the intimate feelings of anyone, no matter whom. We can discuss general instances, principles, ideas, but we have no right to bring into the arena of the press matters relating to the soul and heart of Eusébio, or any other citizen.

On the other hand, it is understandable that we should want Eusébio to be ours, given that he is one of the greatest footballers of all time. Eusébio was the flag that identified Portugal. In the eighties, many in the world still recognized Portugal through its two emblems: Eusébio and Amália Rodrigues. It's therefore natural that we should want Eusébio to be a source of our pride. But there are things that can only be obtained by means of seduction. The heart of a man or a woman doesn't obey the dictates of conscience. No one loves out of duty.

Eusébio's case may be revealing of other illusions. The question is this: why can't black Africans transform themselves into some other "thing"? If there are whites who are African, if there are blacks who are American, why can't black Africans be European? Nowadays, there are hundreds of thousands of blacks who were born in Europe. They have studied, grown up, and absorbed values there. They have become citizens of the countries where they were born. The vast majority will live their whole lives in those countries. They will have European children and grandchildren. And they mustn't fall into the trap of claiming a ghetto for themselves, a kind of second-class citizenship going by the name of "Afro-European." They are European in their own absolute right, they are European not through favour or condescension. They participate in the same process of identity exchange as any other European citizen. Two years ago in France, I fell prey to this stereotyped view of the world. Wherever I went, I saw huge posters of a beautiful black woman. So I asked:

"Is that woman a singer?"

"No, she's Christiane Taubira, and she's running for President of the Republic."

All this, all these stories, are to tell you this: a man isn't a shore, merely existing on one side or the other. A man is a bridge linking various shores. Eusébio can in fact be various things at the same time. Only he can assess to what extent this is true.

Fears and Prejudices

We react with some misgivings to an open discussion about certain questions. One of the topics that scares us is that of nation and ethnicity. Is there such a thing as a Makua nation, a Shona nation, a Zulu nation? Or are they merely ethnic groups? But then what exactly is the difference between these categories? Are we merely debating the meaning of words?

The truth is that, for many of us, these words, these categories, are important points of reference. There isn't a South African Zulu who, from time to time, doesn't feel the urge to reclaim his ethnic identity as being his first nation. Just like the rest of us who, at certain moments, are drawn to wield this or that absolute identity. Nation and ethnic identity can coexist without conflict, as has happened in any number of historical moments. But they are also an opportunity for demagogues and the ambitious to promote their personal or group interests.

The debate about dual nationality in Mozambique has always been contaminated by the assumption that it is about taking up Portuguese nationality alongside Mozambican. The truth, however, is that the issue is much wider than this. We cannot forget the ambivalent and arbitrary history of our frontiers. How many Mozambicans have their history divided between being Mozambicans and Zimbabweans, South Africans, Malawians, Tanzanians, Zambians, Swazis? And there's more to it than that: if we consider that ethnicities were in fact historically defined nations, then it is perfectly natural that a Mozambican citizen may feel he belongs both to the modern Mozambican nation and to the Shona nation. He will always feel "divided" loyalties. This doesn't mean that he is less Mozambican or that he should feel less Mozambican than any other citizen.

I used the term "divided" on purpose. It is an intentional error. I recall the poet José Craveirinha's lesson when referring to his mestizo origin: "I am a shared man, I am not a divided man." This is how we all represent ourselves here, shared and not divided. None of us is a citizen of only one nation. We share ourselves among various worlds. We are citizens of orality, but also of the written word. We are urban and rural. We belong to the nation of tradition and to that of modernity. We sit down in an office chair at a computer and on a floor mat, without feeling out of place with either form of seating. And this is how it must surely be: sharing different worlds without any one of these worlds gaining hegemony over the others.

Mozambique is a nation made up of many nations. It is a supranational nation. And this should sit comfortably within the territorial space of Mozambique, as we have defined it, just as it should sit comfortably within each one of us. We shall, of course, have to be on our guard against certain politicians who will try to turn our differences into levers with which to create division. Let us beware, then, of those who propose crusades in search of purity and authenticity.

Citizenship Without a City?

The origin of the word citizenship is easy to identify: it comes from city. In the same way, "civic spirit" is an expression that comes from *civis*, that which is urban.

In Mozambique, we shall have different and diverse citizenships. But modern citizenship, that which will make us more part of the world, is born in the city. Herein lies a problem, however: to what extent are our cities already urban, both in the cultural sense, and in the sene that their way of life is based on civic responsibility?

Let us take the case of our capital, the city that might serve as a kind of model. For most of its citizens, Maputo is still Xilunguini. What does Xilunguini mean? It's the place where Portuguese is spoken, or in a more generic sense, where people live like whites. When did Maputo turn into a place that is mentally represented as ours, reshaped in accordance with our ways?

The perception Mozambicans have of the cities of southern Mozambique was invented outside Mozambique. It was born from the contact between our miners and country folk and South African cities. The term *doropa* comes from *dorp*, the word that designates a "small town" in Afrikaans.

The history of the city is linked to human processes that we inhabitants of Maputo are unaware of. But it is important to know the history of each one of our cities. That is where the feeling of citizenship begins: one only loves what one knows. And we cannot love our cities if they are seen as legacies left by outsiders.

We have an idea that Mozambique is a rural country, and this is true, but we are rapidly changing from being a rural country to an urban one. Soon (in less than ten years), most of Mozambique's population will live in cities. This will have decisive consequences for our social, economic and environmental policies.

In 1994, around five million Mozambicans lived in cities; in 2025, this population will amount to more than twenty-one million. In other words, in 2025, 61 percent of Mozambicans will live in cities. At that point, the country dwellers will be in the minority. Once again, Mozambique will become something else. Once again, we shall be ambushed by History.

Our Other Poverties

We were taught to attribute fault to others, to find explanations for adversity in foreign enemies. The guilty are those from the South, the North, whites, blacks, Christians, Muslims. We easily embark on a discourse that casts stones and promises to purify the world, repudiating those who are different from ourselves. We need a symbol for the nation that includes those who don't speak the official language well, that doesn't marginalize the illiterate and poorest members of society, and that doesn't privilege or exclude anyone on the basis of race, colour, faith or origin.

We are talking about training in citizenship, and we are thinking about our situation as the inhabitants of a country, but our principal citizenship is that of a nation that lies within each one of us. We often lack the courage to seek out our demons within ourselves. We need to learn to tame our ghosts and overcome our inner fears. I, who am addressing you here, have my own fears, my own anguish. I have brought some of these to your attention, in the form of doubts and aspirations.

My hope, my greatest hope, is that amid so many *workshops* we may learn to know, to recognize, and to resist the demagogy of those who are after votes. There are some things that are resolved by governments, but there are things that no government can resolve. It is we who will resolve them in the time accorded to us, through our developing sense of citizenship.

Mozambique has become the champion for conferences and *workshops*. There's nothing bad about so much "workshopping." But it is dangerous to assume that talking is action. My hope is that, with so many seminars, we may bring ourselves closer to one another in spite of all our differences. And that we may know and acknowledge each other as citizens of a common nation.

As a writer, the Nation that interests me is the human soul. I wrote a book which I called *Every Man is a Race*. I can tell you now: each person is a nation. We here are a kind of assembly of nations. And I feel honoured for having had this opportunity to talk with so many nations, with so many diverse worlds that have come together in the same hope, and knowing that this hope is called the Mozambican nation.

Address to the Tambor Seminar,
Pemba, Mozambique, July, 2004.

THE BRAZILIAN
SERTÃO* IN THE
MOZAMBICAN
SAVANNAH

I SHALL BEGIN with a story. A true story. At the turn of the
nineteenth century, a Mozambican woman by the name of
Juliana lived in the peace and quiet of her little island, and
in the serene contemplation of the waters of the Indian Ocean.
Her life's limited world would be changed one afternoon when
her father, a prosperous merchant called Sousa Mascarenhas,
brought home a sick man. The guest was burning with fever
and in order to ensure his treatment, he was accommodated
in a room in their large townhouse. Juliana became his nurse,
responsible for the intruder's gradual recovery.

During his convalescence, Juliana and the man fell in
love. Juliana's tender care was returned by means of verses
scrawled on loose sheets of paper. Not long afterwards, the
two were married. In the long soirées held in the colonial

---

* The Brazilian backlands or outback

mansion, the educated people of the island would come together and the man would recite his poetry. These soirées witnessed the birth of the first nucleus of poets and writers on Mozambique Island, the first capital of colonial Mozambique. That man was a Brazilian, and his name was António Gonzaga. Years later, he and his beloved Juliana died and were buried in the island's little cemetery.

The birth of Mozambican poetry was heralded by an encounter, or more appropriately, a marriage, between two people. What happened was a premonition of the wider union of minds that would later prevail.

More than a century later, an intellectual trend was born concerned with defining Mozambican identity. By this time, there was a clear need to break with Portugal and European models. Writers such as Rui de Noronha, Noémia de Sousa, Orlando Mendes and Rui Nogar, practised a form of writing that was linked more closely to the land and to the people of Mozambique.

What they needed was a literature that might help them to discover and reveal their native land. Once again, Brazilian poetry came to the assistance of Mozambicans. Manuel Bandeira was possibly the most important figure on this second journey. But Manuel Bandeira wasn't the only one. Along with him came others such as Mário de Andrade, sharing their homeless homeland together, but what they all had in common was a desire to seek out what they called "the Brazilianization of their language." The Mozambicans discovered, in the work of these poets and writers, the possibility of writing in another way, closer to the speech patterns of their homeland, without falling into the temptation of exoticism.

What these writers from Brazil were doing wasn't just a stylistic exercise. Their writing was a result of their willingness to be possessed by and to take possession of Brazilian culture.

It was a question of writing being conquered by speech, and of territories, formerly the preserve of so-called high culture, being flooded by popular culture.

Mário de Andrade wrote, "I care little whether I am writing just as the Portuguese do; what I write is the Brazilian language: for the simple fact that it is my language, the language of my country, Brazil."

Bandeira didn't react against Portugal. He just wanted to forget it. The Brazilians were now yielding to the luxury of forgetfulness. But this detachment from memory wasn't possible in the Mozambican case. Mozambique was still a colony. It was necessary to be "against." How, then, to find in the art of writing, a weapon that promised a fertile future? The question asks for some new encounter, some nourishment with which to gain strength and hope in order to move History forward.

For this, authors such as Graciliano Ramos, Jorge Amado, Rachel de Queiroz and poets like Carlos Drummond de Andrade and João Cabral de Melo Neto, served as sources of inspiration. Mozambique drank from the spirit of another continent. Two oceans couldn't separate what culture and History had made neighbours. Jorge Amado was banned in Portugal, but the Portuguese colonial authorities didn't believe that anyone read in Mozambique. For them, the book was a seed with no soil. They were mistaken in their calculation; the seed germinated and bore fruit. José Craveirinha (our greatest poet, who died recently), Rui Knopfli, Luís Carlos Patraquim and so many others, all confessed to being influenced by him and the distinct way in which Brazil helped us to find our own way forward.

Apart from these writers and their skills, other much more far-reaching, telluric phenomena were occurring. The Mozambican and Brazilian peoples didn't just share the same language but also shared that which developed out of the language, distinguishing it from the Portuguese of Portugal. In both cases, the development of the language was influenced by those of Bantu origin, which introduced affinities between our variant and that of Brazil.

At a deeper level, however, cultural and religious influences were at work. The Brazilian cultural matrix is profoundly influenced by the contribution of African slaves. We tend only to acknowledge isolated aspects of this influence. But its origin is deeper: it embraces the realm of religious thought. Our relationship with the divine is the bedrock of our spirituality, both as individuals and as a collectivity. Although there are clear differences between East and West Africa (from where Brazil received most of its influences), the truth is that we share gods and the same religious logic, far more than we do language and culture.

I shall leave it for others to talk about my own case. My trajectory has been one marked by poetry and I must pay homage to poets such as João Cabral de Melo Neto, Carlos Drummond de Andrade, and above all, Adélia Prado. But my most important influence is essentially João Guimarães Rosa.

João Guimarães Rosa and I

My country contains within it various countries, profoundly divided among a wide variety of social and cultural universes. I am Mozambican, the son of Portuguese immigrants, I lived under the colonial system, I fought for Independence, I lived through radical social change from socialism to capitalism, from the revolution to civil war. I was born in a pivotal period, between a world that was being born and another that was dying: between a country that never was and another that is still being born. This situation of living on a frontier left its mark on me. The two sides of me require a medium, a translator. Poetry came to my rescue to bridge these distant worlds.

And it was poetry that gave me the prose writer, João Guimarães Rosa. When I read him for the first time, I experienced a sensation I had already felt when listening to the storytellers of my childhood. I didn't just read his text, but I also heard the voices of my childhood. Rosa's books drew me out of the written word as if I had suddenly become selectively illiterate. To enter into those texts, I had to undertake an act beyond reading, requiring a verb that as yet has no name.

More than just his invention of words, what struck me was the emergence of a poetry that withdrew me from the world, that made me unexist. It was language in a state of trance, language that fell into a trance like the mediums in magical and religious ceremonies. It was as if there were some deep intoxication that was allowing other languages to take possession of it, just as a dancer does in my country, when he doesn't limit himself to dancing. He prepares for possession by the spirits. The dancer only dances in order to create that divine moment when he can migrate from his own body.

To achieve that relationship with writing, one needs to be a writer. However, at the same time it is crucial to be a non-writer, to submerge oneself in the realm of orality and escape the rationality of the laws of writing, which present writing as the only system of thought. This is the challenge facing the practitioner of an unbalancing act: to have one foot in each world, that of the text and that of the word. It's not just a matter of visiting the world of orality. One needs to allow oneself to be invaded by and fused with the universe of speech, legends, and proverbs. João Guimarães Rosa delayed his entry into the world of writing, and for much of his life, remained a non-writer. As a doctor and a diplomat, he was someone who visited literature but didn't take up permanent residency there.

The storytellers of my country have to follow a ritual when they finish their narration. They have to "close" the story. In "Closing" the story, happens when the narrator speaks to the story itself. It is thought that historical accounts are taken out of a box left behind by Guambe and Dzavane, the first man and first woman. At the end of the ceremony, the narrator turns to the story—as if the story were a protagonist—and tells it: "Go back to the house of Guambe and Dzavane." In this way, the story is shut away back inside the primordial trunk.

What happens when the story isn't "closed"? The crowd of listeners falls ill, struck down by a malady known as dreaming sickness. João Guimarães Rosa is a narrator who didn't close the story. We who listened to him, fell ill. What's more, we fell in love with this illness, this magic, this gift for fantasy.

We are, in fact, in the presence not just of a creator of words, but of a poet who reinvents prose. It's as if there were an earthquake in the heart of writing, a language in a state of trance, just like the African dancer preparing to be possessed. We catch this act at the precise moment when it has ceased being a dance and is becoming the vehicle for exchange between body and soul. A language creating disorder, capable of converting language into the state of initial chaos, is the bearer of the most fundamental upheaval because it is the founder of a new beginning. João Guimarães Rosa is a master: an educator in the unfamiliarities so necessary to us if we are to understand a world that is only legible beyond the borderline of the laws of writing.

Between the Sertão and the Savannah: The Reinvention of Landscape

The *sertão* is an almost untranslatable word. Dominated by the arid plains and barren lands of the interior, it gives its name to one of the poorest regions of Brazil. Embracing more than a third of the country's territory (larger than many European countries), the sertão is not, however, a geographical term. "The sertão," Guimarães Rosa said, "is within us."

The sertão is therefore a world in the process of being invented. All this can be said about the savannah, the space where the African landscape is not only constructed but also defined. The sertão and the savannah are thus worlds constructed in language. Within these territories the reader is both the journey and the traveller. However, although these territories invite us to walk within them, they are not spaces that one crosses. For Rosa, the sertão is, itself, the crossing ("crossing" in fact being the word that closes his novel, *The Devil to Pay in the Backlands*).

What grips us when we read Rosa is what he pursued in his writing, "that moving, intractable, disturbing thing that rebels against any logic," that thing that declares itself in the silence of the sertão, in the portent of the path ahead, in the poetry that is a journey from the desert to the oasis.

It is important to place João Guimarães Rosa's work in its historical context. Books such as *The Devil to Pay in the Backlands* were written as Brazilians witnessed the birth of a capital city, where previously there was nothing, right in the middle of the sertão (Brasília had just been built); this completed a process of centralized control over that multiple and elusive reality. In truth, the sertão was mythologized in order to counter certain aspirations toward homogeneity and modernization in the emergent Brazil. Rosa doesn't write about the sertão. He writes *as if* he were the sertão. A sertão full of stories to counter the course of History.

One needs to abandon reason in order to look at this Brazil which Guimarães Rosa shows us, as if in order to touch reality, a certain hallucinatory gift were necessary, a madness capable of redeeming the invisible. Writing isn't a vehicle for arriving at an essence. Writing is the journey, the discovery of other dimensions and mysteries that lie beyond appearances. "When nothing happens, there is a miracle that we cannot see."

The Devil to Pay in the Backlands reveals a political positioning, not because it is constructed on the basis of an ideology, but because, in its very language, João Guimarães Rosa suggests a utopia, a future beyond what he denounces as an attempt at an "improved form of destitution." His language, which mediates between that of the educated classes and that of the backlands country folk, didn't exist in Brazil. Through his collective form of writing, João Guimarães Rosa presents a Brazil in which the marginalized might take part in the invention of its History.

And here, we reach a way forward that will enable us to share one of the few certainties that Rosa left us: what a writer gives us isn't books. What he gives us through his writing is a world. We were unaware of that world, and yet it existed within us as a silent memory of some lost enchantment. The light and shadow of the page already lay dormant within us. In a sense, reading reawakens that enchantment for us. That is the sensation felt when we discover the written work of João Guimarães Rosa.

One Work Against the Whole Oeuvre

Guimarães Rosa turned his back on an oeuvre. He refused to make a career out of literature. What interested him without a doubt was the intensity of an experience that bordered on the religious. Three of his books were published posthumously. The important thing for Rosa wasn't the books but the act of writing itself.

In his *Poetics of Music,* Stravinsky wrote: "We have a duty toward music, namely, to invent it." The writer's duty towards language is to recreate it, rescuing it from the process of trivialization established by common usage. For Guimarães Rosa, language needed to "flee from the inflexibility of commonplace expression, escape from viscosity, from somnolence." It wasn't simply a matter of aesthetics, but, as far as he was concerned, it had to do with the very meaning of writing. He wanted to explore the potential of language, by challenging conventional narrative processes, and allowing the written word to be penetrated by myth and by orality.

In this way, Rosa carried out a project to free writing from the weight of its own rules. To achieve this, he made use of everything: neologisms, disrupted catchphrases, reinvented proverbs, and reclaimed material from oral culture placing all of it not merely in footnotes, but at the heart of the text.

Word magic and the narration magic are not two separate processes. Guimarães Rosa works outside common sense (he creates an uncommon sense), he evokes the deep mystery in simple things, he gives us the pure quality behind everyday concerns.

This fascination with the creative power that a reinvented language can exert over us was expressed by Rosa when he wrote about Hungarian: "From his earliest understanding of it, every Hungarian writer aspires to create his own 'language,' with its own vocabulary and syntax, its written personality. More than this: it is almost impossible for every Hungarian writer not to have his own, personal idiom. Its range is magical." Perhaps it is no coincidence that Chico Buarque makes himself an apprentice and a writer in Hungarian in his 2003 novel, *Budapest*.

A narration's territory isn't a place, but consists of the journey itself. Its discourse is in constant mutation and the different characters are different voices in dialogue. Narration isn't the privilege of one sole entity, invested with the responsibility of organizing the wisdom and knowledge of others. Riobaldo isn't just the protagonist-narrator of *The Devil to Pay in the Backlands*, but a kind of smuggler between literature, urban culture, and the oral culture of the inhabitants of the sertão. In his writing, João Guimarães Rosa undertakes a fusion of feelings and meanings, a bridge between modernity and rural tradition, between the modern epic form and the logic of the traditional story. This, at heart, is Brazil itself.

This is the challenge behind the unceasing search for a pluralistic identity that still faces Brazil. Mozambique faces the same challenge. More than a turning point, what we need today is a medium, someone who uses powers that don't come from science or technology, in order to connect these different universes. What we need is to be connected with those whom Rosa called "the folk on the far side." That side is within each and every one of us.

Address to the Brazilian Academy of Letters,
Rio de Janeiro, August 2004.

ANIMAL CONSERVATION: A NOAH-LESS ARK?

Introduction

I'T'S BAD FORM to begin with a question. Yet I have no choice but to share my first concern with you: when we discuss matters relating to conservation and tourism, do we know exactly what we are talking about?

This is an area in which words and concepts are a slippery, moving pavement. *Conservation, ecotourism, local communities, participatory management of natural resources*: all these are concepts that need to be questioned. They reach us like some imported fruit: we must peel them, taste them and judge whether they will be productive in our own soil. It's not a question of refusing influences or closing our doors against global trends. The question is: How we can build our own agenda from fragments of others' agendas.

I have to confess I feel some misgivings about beginning this talk in such a way, given that it may provoke a certain apathy among us all. We can't remain indecisive on the grounds that we don't know enough. We don't have the right to such a

luxury. However, worse than not having knowledge is thinking that one does. That's why I've chosen to speak to you
about mistakes, simplifications, and mystifications.

1. Philosophical Fallacies:
Dancing Words and Flying Concepts

I have already had occasion to recount this true incident:
some years ago, President Chissano presented the members
of his government at a political rally in Nampula. His speech
was in Portuguese, but translated into Makua. When he got to
the point of introducing his Minister of Culture, the translator hesitated and said: This is the Minister of Jokes.

All of us have experienced this kind of misunderstanding.
In most of our Bantu languages, there isn't a translation for
the word "culture," just as there isn't a translation for "nature,"
or for "society." This absence of an equivalent term doesn't
stem from any inadequacy among our languages. Rather, it
comes from a different philosophical stance, another vision of
the world. For most rural Mozambicans there isn't a frontier
dividing that which is "cultural" from that which is "natural."
What there is is an interconnected world, that can only be
understood and defined in one way.

What we need to remember is that our discussion today is
not based on a holistic view of the world, but on a dualistic philosophy propounded by Descartes in the first half of the seventeenth century, from which strong dichotomies later evolved:
between "natural" and "social," between "conservation" and
"utilization," between "man" and "nature." We remain prisoners of false conflicts, between the "exploitation" and "preser-
vation" of that which is "impure" and "virgin," between that
which has been "transformed" and that which is "untouched."

There never has been a natural world that hasn't included
the participation of human societies; uncultivated vegetation

has always occurred with human interference (for at least the last 250,000 years). We were intervening in the ecological process long before there were workshops on tourism and conservation. We are both a product and the producers of our environment. We are both nature and society.

I'm talking of words and concepts, some of which appear and contest each other like passing fashions. If we aren't careful, we may merely be dressing what are really much older concepts in new words. For example, "local communities" may be a new name for what began by being known as "natives," in order to later become "indigenous people," and then later "peasant masses," and still more recently the "population."

2. The Fallacies of History

When we talk about the environment in Mozambique, we often lose historical perspective, as if everything began with colonialism. We know almost nothing about the environmental changes that occurred during our pre-colonial past. We never study the impact made by the communities of iron makers, or of agricultural practices inspired by the use of fire, in phenomena such as the Mfecane, which brought waves of Nguni migration to the south of Mozambique.

The model for the term we now call "conservation" was born during the British Empire in the middle of the eighteenth century. During that period, there were the first signs of severe industrial pollution and urban growth. A nostalgia for "pure," "virgin" Nature became predominant, as did a perceived need to protect natural spaces as if they were fortresses. For these territories to be restored to their "natural" state, all human presence was to be withdrawn, and they were to be protected by guarded enclosures. In the end, they were trying to recreate a lost paradise, to re-enact the biblical myth of Noah's Ark.

Reserves, parks and botanical gardens were created during the course of that century in various parts of the empire,
from the East Indies to the Cape. Our region witnessed the
birth, in 1892, of the Sabie Game Reserve. After this, various
other conservation areas emerged in southern Africa.

Most parks emerged first as estates or reserves for game
hunting. This happened throughout the world. It happened in
Mozambique as well. This means that our current conservation areas were not chosen originally on the basis of ecological
or sociological criteria, or for the protection of biodiversity.

It's not just Bantu languages that have difficulty express-
ing certain concepts. This difficulty also exists among
European languages. It is no coincidence that the translation
of certain English terms like *wildlife, wilderness, or pristine*
have no easy equivalent in other languages. This is because
these concepts are native to England, and spread within the
framework of the British Empire. The English were on a campaign to return to nature, but without ever becoming incorporated into it. They were educated visitors, separated by
their civilization from primitive peoples. Even hunting in
Europe was ritualized in order to throw the virtues of the
noble horseman into relief against the cruel barbarity of the
impoverished country folk.

Conservationism was marked by social discrimination
from its inception. Later on, within the colonial context, racism provided new chapters for this classical narrative. The
Europeans hunted for sport, while the Africans were limited to hunting furtively. The Europeans were hunters, while
the Africans were poachers.

The first government departments for the protection of
fauna were created to defend colonial reserves from threats
posed by local populations and these furtive hunters. Africa
was always seen as the lost paradise, and progress as an
implacable destroyer. Africa always was the epicentre of this
idyllic vision of Nature. Books such as *A Lioness Called Elsa*

and *Serengeti Shall Not Die* became bestsellers as early as the 1960s. Nowadays, television documentaries about wild fauna serve to champion conservation among the viewing public.

Such mystification isn't all bad, for its facile, reductive vision is today one of the most potent factors in attracting tourists.

It is no coincidence that we designate parks as "sanctuaries." The religious terminology isn't innocent or casual. Rather, it reflects an updating of Europe's missionary vocation in our continent. We already have paradise, which is "savage" Africa; we have the devil, which is progress. We have the sinners: all of us who give in to the temptation of "development." All we need is salvation—the salvation known as "environmental conservation."

In the meantime, African countries have become independent, and those who were poachers have become environmentalists. Colonial departments for the protection of fauna have been incorporated into national policies. The African elites have assumed, with one or two adjustments, the vision from past times. From this point on, European mystifications about Africa have become African ones as well. We haven't just nationalized assets and the soil. We have nationalized concepts. Yet this in itself isn't a sin—to borrow again from religious terminology—as long as we develop our awareness and create our own forms of thinking.

Independence brought with it a thirst for modernization. An army of scientists, planners, and agricultural developers, threw itself into a campaign for change based on a simplified vision in which the land was divided into two categories:

arable zones, destined for agriculture;

marginal zones, destined for livestock farming.

Within this set-up, animals would live in the game reserves. And the people would live in the space left between reserves.

We therefore inherited a view of conservation that was based on the strategy of the fortress. Now, we are being bombarded by a kind of counterpoint to this discourse, which is centred on Nature. This bombardment is called "community involvement." The discourse concerning communities aims to end the exclusion of people in the physical, political sense. These new ideas have emerged within the context of another much wider current of thought, which is that concerning the sustainable management of resources, a current originating in the United States in the middle of the twentieth century.

These two tendencies (that of the fortress and that of the community) are not as different as they might seem: the first is biocentric, the second is anthropocentric. There are those who complain that the second route—that of community involvement—is a kind of bleaching agent, a way of cleaning and giving a moral edge to the first route. There is and must be a considereable amount of internal debate about this, that we are doing here today.

Part of the mystification of African history derives from films, where the natives have always been the baddies; environmental predators, however, haven't always been those who were (or are) the poorest. There are documented cases of huge massacres being carried out by Europeans (even if they were done in the name of science). In some regions of Mozambique, the Movement to Combat Sleeping Sickness killed more than 233,000 mammals of 45 different species over a period of twelve years. Not even rare species in danger of extinction, such as rhinos, cheetahs, tsessebe, roan antelope, and giraffes were spared. In the neighbouring areas of Massangena and Govuro alone, 180,000 animals were destroyed. These campaigns, though the subject of criticism, went on until the country's independence in 1975.

And there were even cases when local chiefs and rulers defined areas of conservation, and imposed hunting restrictions on Europeans. These were isolated instances, but they reveal an inversion of the logic governing the relationship between predators and conservationists. Shaka Zulu, for example, created a reserve for the members of his court, in what is now the Umfolozi Park. A conservation area was created by the Shangaan groups who left Mozambique and settled in the present-day region of the Gonarezhou National Park. King Mzilikazi began to require European hunters wishing to hunt in parts of what is now Zimbabwe to seek his special authorization.

3. *The Fallacy of Violence: Other Less Visible Crimes*

Colonial violence towards rural communities didn't just occur when they expelled people from the parks. More subtle means of violence occurred along with other, less visible forms of exclusion, including:

economic models that forced dramatic changes in the management of the soil and its resources;

disturbances of rural society in relation to the logic of a centralized State;

devaluations of local language, culture, practical knowledge and religion.

Nor where these mechanisms for exclusion confined to areas of conservation. They were common throughout the colonized territory. In some sense, all communities in Mozambique were dislocated. They were dislocated from their way of life, their language, their culture, their religion. Some of these mechanisms are still present today. It is important for us to be aware of this.

There were other forms of violence that were far less visible. The case of the Selous Game Reserve in Tanzania is an example. In 1905, the communities living in an area of the Maji-Maji district revolted against the colonial administration. The strategy adopted by the German authorities was not to crush the revolt militarily, but to drive the rebellious population to exhaustion and famine. Around 300,000 Tanzanians were killed. Germany described the ensuing situation as being one of "peace." An extensive area had thus been emptied and all they now needed to do was to withdraw another 40,000 inhabitants to establish the largest park in Africa.

Profound ecological imbalances were used to displace inhabitants from regions that were to be converted into conservation areas. Bovine disease was one of the more insidious of such mechanisms. The historian John Reader classified bovine disease as the greatest calamity of all time in the whole continent. In a mere eleven years, from 1889 to 1900, 90-95 percent of Africa's domestic livestock died. Without cattle, the population obviously died too. Two thirds of the Masai population disappeared. And so a chain reaction of imbalances occurred: areas of pasture were invaded by trees and other woody vegetation, new areas for the expansion of the tsetse fly were created, and the incidence of sleeping sickness increased, causing more cattle to die. But above all, it caused more people to die. More than 200,000 country dwellers died in Uganda alone.

4. Science and Its Fallacies: Questioning Certainties

The misuse of science helps to entrench prejudices. We have the idea that "pure," "untouched" nature is that which corresponds to the climax of an ecological succession: an ecosystem is in its "natural," "balanced" state when we have a lot of vegetation, lots of trees, and a lot of fauna. The concepts of "balance" and "natural" do not correspond to the reality of the dynamics between man and the environment. There is nothing—and current science tells us this—but states of balance at particular points and temporary situations of stability.

One of the concepts that has earned considerable criticism is that of the so-called "load capacity." The idea was reproduced from models for the management of pasture for domestic cattle in the United States. We now believe this concept was transferred to the ecosystems of the savannah without taking into account climate variation and the interrelationship between herbivores, soil and vegetation in African biomes.

Our scientists are profoundly contaminated by this destructive separation between "natural" and "anthropogenic" environments. The vast majority of our specialists are not equipped to understand the natural and social mechanisms at work in the savannah. We have hydraulic engineers to see to questions of irrigation, and we have hydrologists who know about artificial systems. We have few if any hydrologists working on natural systems. Our forestry experts look at a tree for its timber. Our veterinary experts work on dogs and oxen, but we have few who know how to handle wildlife. We have a shortage of ecologists, sociologists and anthropologists who know about the mechanisms and dynamics of our rural world.

We need economists to assess the monetary value of our resources, our trees and animals. Otherwise, how will we be able to compare the best options for our use of the land, among which features the option for tourism?

5. *The Mirror and Its Misrepresentation: Overestimating Our Potential*

There is a certain naïve optimism when we assess our potential in relation to tourism. I am in permanent contact with reports by Mozambican experts who very often point to the regions of the Mozambican interior as containing huge potential for tourism. They don't ask themselves who will come, or where they will stay . . .

This optimism stands in contrast to other more pessimistic attitudes. Chinua Achebe is possibly one of the most illustrious living African writers. He is a Nigerian, and has been a candidate for the Nobel Prize for Literature on a number of occasions. Speaking of his country in 1984, he didn't mince words: "Nigeria is one the most disorderly nations in the world. It is one of the most corrupt, insensitive, inefficient places under the sun. It is one of the most expensive countries and one of those that give least value for money. It is dirty, callous, noisy, ostentatious, dishonest and vulgar."

When asked about the possibilities of Nigeria developing its tourist industry, the same writer replied:

"It is a measure of our self-delusion that we can talk about developing tourism in Nigeria. Only a masochist with an exuberant taste for self-violence will pick Nigeria for a holiday; only a character out of Tutuola seeking to know punishment and poverty first-hand! No, Nigeria may be a paradise for adventurers and pirates, but not tourists."

Our future may be that of Nigeria. But it could also be the opposite: that of Mauritius, Tunisia, Morocco.

We need to view our country's potential in light of ecotourism's intensely competitive market. In 1996, there were 30,361 parks and conservation areas in the whole world. These areas of conservation covered a total of 13,243,528 square kilometres (that is, 8 percent of the total area of the planet). A tourist can choose from a territory that is collectively about seventeen times larger than Mozambique. Our attractions have to compete with this vast range of choices.

Our ingenuousness in the appreciation of our potential isn't in itself a bad thing—but it obscures the direction we need to take in order to transform potential into a proper tourist destination.

We live in a world characterized by contingency and unpredictability. Kenya and Tanzania were the most attractive tourist destinations in our region. The 1998 bomb attacks by Al-Qaeda had a profound effect on tourist numbers. Kenya lost $13.5 million, or 20 percent of its tourist revenue. Around 10,000 workers lost their jobs.

The case of Zimbabwe is even more revealing: until 1999, tourism was the fastest-growing industry in the country, contributing 8.3 percent to its GNP. After Robert Mugabe's so-called "agrarian reform," Zimbabwe lost $582 million in three years in the area of tourism alone. In the first two years, the movement of tourists decreased by 40 percent. But the damage wasn't limited to this: the so-called "war veterans" occupied the parks and embarked on an indiscriminate massacre of the wildlife. In just one conservation area known as the Save Valley Conservation—an area covering 3,400 square kilometres—these "war vets" killed 1600 animals in only six months. 340 kilometres of electric fencing were transformed into tens of thousands of trip wires for traps.

The fluid character of the political reality has to be taken into account. Today, a huge percentage of tourists come from South Africa. If the same thing that happened in Zimbabwe happens in South Africa (even though this may only be a remote possibility), how will it affect our tourism and our economy?

6. *The Misrepresentation of Communities and of Noble Savages*

We have already seen that misunderstandings are abundant in all areas. However, when people talk about communities, there is an endless collection of fallacies and naïve views. These much-discussed communities only become visible when viewed through an ethnic or anthropological prism. With a bit of luck, we shall see that they are no more than fictitious entities, blurred by a sum of stereotypes and preconceptions. I shall now talk about these myths:

Myth 1—Identity

No one knows exactly what a community is. No one knows who forms part of this collectivity, or what family or genea-logical networks are included in each specific case. We are confronting a stereotype that doesn't respect diversity, or the complex nature of social dynamics. We need to acknowledge this: communities are not homogeneous or egalitarian. They are marked by social conflicts, based on power, on gender. And more than anything, they are composed of segments that have varied and sometimes conflicting interests.

Most of the time, rather than communities, we see an army of NGOs, which presents itself as civil society, and which speaks in the name of a rural population that remains out of the picture and invisible.

Myth 2—Harmony With the Environment

The idea exists that communities only develop balanced, har-monious relationships with the environment. This is not true. For many centuries now, many so-called traditional practices have entered into conflict with the environment and have become sources of aggression and imbalance.

Some conservation practices and examples of balanced resource management corresponded to historical periods when there was low population density, less mobility, and above all when there wasn't the population pressure that exists nowadays.

We are justified in our criticism of the fortress policy in relation to parks. But, in fairness, we have to accept that this policy has preserved spaces in which wildlife might still be found.

Myth 3—Purity

We nurture the illusion that communities are above suspi-cion of robbery or corruption. Sadly this is not the case; the community is part of this system, and where there is money, there is temptation and bribery. Only last year, I took part in a debate within one of these communities, in which its members denounced a string of abuses perpetrated by their leaders, involving the undue appropriation of funds to acquire luxury goods. I won't mention the name of this community but I can assure you that it is widely held up as an example of the apparent success of the policy of community involvement.

Myth 4—Poverty and the Success of Community Policies

There is no doubt that the uprooting of communities to create spaces for wildlife was a historical injustice that did irreparable damage. But one also has to admit that the poverty of these communities is not greatly different from that of other rural communities, which were never expelled from their original areas.

We must look at the acclaimed success of community projects with a critical eye. Many which served as flag-bearers are today experiments that have failed.

Myth 5—The State's Abdication from Responsibility

The discourse about communities coincides with external neo-liberal pressure to reduce the role and responsibility of the State. If we do not wish local communities to adopt a predatory attitude towards resources, we must prioritize investment in the adjoining areas, which are the parks. The State, if it wants returns, must give priority to infrastructures, roads and services. Until now, we have assumed that this task must fall exclusively to the individual investor in such regions. But no investor can promote the whole range of activities, cover general shortages, correct regional imbalances *and* fulfill the role of the government.

The State cannot delude itself into thinking it can hand the initiative over to private investors and pass supervision of this over to the NGOs. *The State should not be asked to do less, but it should be asked to do other things*, such as taking the initiative, planning, regulating, supervising, controlling.

Myth 6—*The Marginalization of Local Government Authorities*

If the State at the level of the central government is on a diet, at the district level, it is training for total abolition. In the districts, as if by some stroke of wizardry that I have never understood, there is practically no government authority. What there is, are NGOs, local communities, and traditional leaders.

It should be the reverse. We shall, in fact, only have strong communities if there is consolidated local government, technically prepared to face issues of conservation and development. The local administration of a district or an area next to a park should know how the process of integrated management of its wildlife actually works. What is more, it should have such management as its principal aim.

Myth 7—*Between Paternalism and the Feeling of Guilt*

The communities adjoining parks should, of course, be involved, but we need to ask ourselves how and on what basis. Allow me to ask a mischievous question: in the management of an airport, how would you involve the neighbouring communities, would you turn them into profit-sharers or co-administrators? Of course not. An airport is an area with technically sophisticated specialist needs. Well let me tell you that the management of ecotourism or the use of resources for tourism is an equally specific area with highly sophisticated technical requirements.

And then of course we need to study rigorously (and above all without any demagogic agenda) the experiences of others. I have seen studies made by Europeans that maintain that the invasion of parks by communities is legitimate because it is a question of historic vengeance for their exclusion during colonial and post-colonial times. Is this really the case? Or will it always be like this? Were the war veterans in Zimbabwe, who attacked the parks, really the neighbouring communities? One thing seems true: we cannot stand here with arms folded, and escape our obligation to protect a national patrimony merely out of guilt.

In all these cases, when we talk of communities, we invent an entity that doesn't exist. If we want current communities to be effective partners in our politics of development, with greater equity and efficiency, we shall have to create them. We cannot wait for these communities to reveal themselves spontaneously. We need a government program that will enable these communities to constitute themselves. Otherwise, with the paternalism that drives us currently, we will eventually offer these rural populations a poisoned chalice.

Final Conclusion

My friends, it is not merely a question of reconciling tourism and conservation. It is a question of reconciling agriculture, forestry, livestock farming, and all forms of governance with the changing reality of Mozambique and of the World. It is certainly a question of reconciling all aspects of the State's intervention with the reality of rural Mozambique.

The difficulties we have in wildlife conservation are not very different from those experienced in the fields of agriculture, or of mineral extraction, or in other areas of development. We still have difficulties of a cultural nature. The question of conservation (or rather, of the sustainable management of natural resources), will only become a political reality after it has become a cultural reality. Let me ask you this: how many of our leaders have visited or had any contact with a park or reserve inside or outside Mozambique? These experiences need to be lived. Only after contact with wildlife, and only after ecotourism has become a fact of culture, will these matters cease to be a secondary concern in our manner of governance.

We are the inheritors of Noah's Ark. But we are an impoverished Noah, at risk of extinction both as sovereign nations and as people exercising their citizenship. Some want us to act as saviours of our natural patrimony. Others want us to build a new Ark, an improved Ark, with luxury cabins for a wealthy minority. It isn't an Ark we need. What we need is another world, a world that doesn't live under threat of a final deluge.

Lecture on the conservation of fauna in Mozambique,
as part of a debate promoted by the Terra Viva Centre,
Maputo, June, 2004.

WATERS OF
MY BEGINNING

A CITY isn't a place. It is the frame of a life. A frame in search of a portrait, that's what I see when I revisit my place of birth. It's not streets, or houses. What I see again is a time, what I hear is the speech of that time. A dialect called memory, in a nation called childhood.

In spite of everything, a map puts us at ease: there is the city, the second biggest in Mozambique. That's where concrete, iron, asphalt, the usual vestments of an urban space, were instated. But all this wasn't enough to dismantle the illusion: what dwells in the place of my childhood is the untameable, that which will forever remain ungovernable.

I speak of my Beira, the little city where I was born, located in the centre of Mozambique, on the left bank of the River Pungué. Beira is a place that was stolen from the waters of an estuary, lined with mud and mangroves. A liquid city, on a ground that flows. So much so that when speaking of it, I call it my native water.

Here is the prime example of its audacity: the settlement built on marshland earned the name of a prince. It was named after an obscure Portuguese nobleman—the Prince of Beira, somewhere in Portugal. But at least he was a prince. The people of Beira never knew the identity of this patron whom they had to thank for giving their city its name. The city was invented out of shadows, beginning with its name.

To create a city on land flooded by the tides isn't just a mistake in urban planning—it's utopic, a million-to-one bet. Was Beira dreamt up by an anarchitect?

A Place of Fiction

Small towns dream of being something else. They dream of being villages, or they aspire to be great cities. My hometown was an introverted place, where the world arrived second hand.

We were a place in dispute with the world, and we needed to affirm ourselves in order to exist. The capital, Lourenço Marques, was our shadow. What we had that was good wasn't just good: it was the best. We had the best airport, the best train station, the best sense of community. Whatever weakness we had was compensated for by our collective ability to create fiction about ourselves.

Had Lourenço Marques built a bullring? Well, without any bulls, we invented bullfights and bullfighters. Lourenço Marques had South Africa? Well Beira had Rhodesia. But this proximity merely aggravated our fictional condition: Rhodesia was a country that didn't exist, an entity seeking some impossible recognition. In this struggle to invent itself, my hometown was turned into my first book, with it I learned the pleasure of creating roots that were, at the same time, the wings of my imagination.

I remember the colonial houses, ringed by verandas on all sides, offering little by way of defence against the surrounding continent. Africa was there, impossible to avoid or deny, giving us our hybrid soul. In the evening, as the sun went down, I would go out and sit under the huge mango trees. Bats would flutter swiftly through the air and the houses were bathed in a kind of nostalgia. Beira, which proclaimed itself "the city of the future," in the end, appeared not to want to be a city. Much less a future. As if the place bemoaned its terrain, as if it were avoiding its destiny. As if it knew that, in order to reach the future it claimed for itself, the city would have to correct the distance that separated the concrete town from its reed shanties, and the centre from its impoverished suburbs.

Among Herons and Vultures

It wasn't the time of day that counted there. What time and men wanted to know was the cycle of tides. My parents would warn me when I should get home:

"Make sure you come home before the tide!"

The city was governed by tides, and the tides were controlled by the birds. That's what people said. A little grey bird summoned the tide in. Another bigger one, with white wings, called the tide to go out. I was fascinated by the power of such simple little creatures to command the huge ocean. I wasn't guided by a clock. As a child, I lived like those birds that wait for the waves.

The birds were always my postmen, messengers awaiting a message. In Beira, flamingos, herons, and storks, didn't inhabit the periphery: they patrolled the centre of town, pecking at little bits and pieces in the mud. And I asked myself: were birds all long-legged, or was our ground too low?

Today, I have plenty of experience of visiting other countries. I've become acquainted with many of the world's oldest and most genuine cities, and in all of them, I have noticed the inevitable presence of pigeons. In squares, on pavements, on balconies, pigeons are proof of a city's authenticity, a measure of its degree of urbanization.

Beira didn't have pigeons: it had herons. Like white hand-kerchiefs flying from an invisible mast, the herons revealed a territory guided by a logic that as yet scarcely pertained to humans. There were also flamingos, storks, pelicans. And above all, there were vultures circling in the sky, reeling over the slaughterhouse. These birds of prey fought each other for the leftovers of our future meals. In what other city might one have witnessed such complicity?

The Sea Dripping Memories

There weren't any pigeons and, also, there was no fear. Along with pigeons, fear is another indicator of the extent of urban-ization. And it was without any fear that I would return home, when night had already fallen, along paths that hugged the ocean shore. My bare feet trod the landward side of dark-ness. Our walking barefoot reflected the influence of our Rhodesian neighbours. The "beefsteaks," as we used to call them. But I wasn't aware of this. My feet felt the skin of the soil as we acknowledged each other with a mutual caress.

Our house was on the edge of a wide beach. I would choose the back steps but didn't get as far as the garden door. I would dally in the servants' hut, sharing their mealie flour. My fin-gers were my cutlery mixing the flour with the dried fish sauce. Tired and smelling of curry, I would sink into the folds of the bedsheet as if being welcomed by waves. In the living room, the Bahian, Dorival Caymmi, sang "it's sweet to die at sea." My parents would watch the flamingoes flying into the setting sun. For me, the life we led was the stuff of poetry.

I recall ghosts from my childhood to show how my home-town never freed itself from the sea, how it remained subject to a delicate harmony between Nature and Man.

Now, as I sleep, there is no scene that doesn't contain the ocean in it. The Macúti lighthouse persists as a solitary sentinel, striped black and white like a zebra's leg. The mangroves of Praia Nova resist like salty veins, irrigating the body of my memory. The little boats—the pirogues and dinghies—ride the muddy waters of my forgetfulness. The Indian Ocean became my soul's shore. It was out there that I was born. So much so that nowadays my dreams are amphibian. The past is a shore where everything turns to foam. And my hometown is made of sea air and spume.

Dualities, Enlightenment

But it wasn't just memories that Beira gave me. The city taught me how my country has various countries within it, scattered deeply between varied social and cultural worlds.

Beira always had difficulty organizing its space in the colonial manner. It was inundated by unmanageable rains, and bordered by impenetrable mangroves. In such circumstances, it was difficult to expel Africa from the place. The settlers would like to have pushed the Africans far away. But the blacks invariably remained there, on the other side of the street. My hometown was doomed to be a borderland—between the sea and the continent, between Europe and Africa, between Catholicism and the religions of the ancestors.

Deep down, the city and I shared the same condition: we were both creatures of the frontier. I am Mozambican, the son of Portuguese immigrants, I was born at the height of the colonial system, fought for Independence, lived through radical changes from socialism to capitalism, from revolution to the civil war. I was born at a pivotal time, between a world that was nascent and another that was dying. Between a nation that never was and another that is coming to be. The city is an umbilical cord that we create after we have been born.

I grew up in this hybrid environment, listening to the old storytellers. They brought me the magic of a sacred moment.

I was the son of an atheist poet, and that was my first mass, a message from the divine.

I wanted to know who the authors were of those stories and the answer was always the same: no one. It was the ancestors who had created those tales, and the stories remained as the legacy of the gods. The elders were buried right there in the soil, conferring both history and religion upon our relationship with them. In such a dwelling place, the ancestors turn into divine entities.

The moment had a contradictory effect on me: on the one hand, it nurtured me, while on the other, it excluded me. I couldn't share entirely in that conversation between gods and men. I was already burdened with Europe, my soul had already imbibed a way of thinking, and my dead resided in other soil.

When I ask myself why I write, I answer: to get to know gods that aren't mine. My ancestors are buried somewhere else far away, somewhere in the north of Portugal. I don't share their intimacy, and what is still more serious, they have no knowledge of my existence.

My two sides demanded an intermediary, a translator. Poetry came to my rescue, to create a bridge between two worlds. And the city, my home, my family: these nurtured the poetry that was born in me.

An Unsuccessful Escape

In 1972, I left Beira to go and study medicine in Lourenço Marques. There, I settled in like someone disembarking from his own adolescence; for the first time, I was leaving my home behind and facing "life" on my own. This change of locality helped me to understand the various Mozambiques contained within Mozambique. My Chissena was little use to me. The south speaks other languages. Other cultures were produced within a very different historical framework.

I lived through the last four years Lourenço Marques went by that name. I witnessed the deep changes that led not just to another name for the city, but another reality. Ever since then, Mozambican cities have had to create their own urban space from the inside. Urban space was (and still is to some extent) the space reserved for the others, the whites and assimilated Africans. With Independence, urban space tended to become more Mozambican. Cities were occupied progressively, not just by people who arrived from the countryside, but by rural life itself.

Lourenço Marques, however, didn't draw me away from my hometown. In both places, I witnessed how the rural soul takes possession of cities and appropriates a network of relationships that is foreign to it, and what is more, that is contrary to its spirit. This is the tension that exists in Beira and in all African cities. Beira was constructed initially according to a different type of logic. It emerged as a transplant of Europe on foreign soil. The continent's body received these insertions without converting to the rationale behind this. But beyond this tension, there was a certain seduction that the rural world was unable to resist.

Mozambican cities are almost all of recent construction and, until 1975, they were administered according to a foreign modes of thought. They were cities *in* Mozambique, and not cities *of* Mozambique. Nowadays, the urban spirit has only partially become woven into the first generation of Mozambicans born and brought up in cities. This process of appropriation by the city is still going on. And it will take various generations.

Inventing Destinies

Beira, like all our cities, wasn't born "ours." It became ours gradually. One of the dynamics that turned it into a Mozambican space was migration. Beira is a space of arrival. People enter the city as if they were crossing a frontier. On this side lies citizenship, the place where cultures are made and exchanged and where, with much greater intensity, a sense of Mozambicanness is forged.

The city isn't just a physical space but a location where relationships are welded together. It is the focal point of a time when Mozambique's own identities are made and remade. Nor, as a native of Beira, am I the only one to be permeated by dualities. All Mozambican citizens share this same condition: they navigate between cultures, forever adapting to enable more lasting political exchanges that are ideologically more convincing, technologically more well thought out, and socially more promising.

In the end, we don't have much more than this: the city of our childhood. We talk in capital letters of the Nation, the Country, the Global Village. These are ideas. We don't live in them. Nowadays, I don't even yearn for a city. What fills me with yearning is a tiny urban area, a wall where I can once again sit with my childhood friends. And Beira, my Beira, the one I remember from my unfinished childhood, that's the place invented to fit my dream and my nostalgia.

Published by the Casa Fernando Pessoa, Lisbon, Portugal, in *Tabacaria*, October, 2003.

LANGUAGES WE
DON'T KNOW WE KNOW

I N   A N   A S - Y E T - U N P U B L I S H E D   short story of mine, the
action is as follows: a terminally ill woman asks her husband to tell her a story so as to alleviate her unbearable
pains. No sooner does he begin his tale than she stops him:

"No, not like that. I want you to speak to me in an
unknown language."

"Unknown?" he asks.

"A language that doesn't exist. For I have such a need not
to understand anything at all."

The husband asks himself: how can you speak a language
that doesn't exist? He starts off by mumbling some strange
words and feels like a fool, as if he were proving to himself his
inability to be human. But gradually, he begins to feel more
at ease with this language that is devoid of rules. And he no
longer knows whether he's speaking, singing, or praying.
When he pauses, he notices his wife has fallen asleep, with the
most peaceful smile on her face. Later, she confesses to him:
those sounds had brought back memories of a time before she
even had a memory! And they had given her the solace of that
same sleep which provides the link between us and what was
here before we were alive.

When we were children, all of us experienced that first language, the language of chaos, all of us enjoyed that divine moment when our life was capable of being all lives, and the world still awaited a destiny. James Joyce called this relationship with an unformed, chaotic world "chaosmology." This relationship, my friends, is what breathes life into writing, whatever the continent, whatever the nation, whatever the language or the literary genre.

I believe that all of us, whether poets or fiction writers, never stop seeking this seminal chaos. All of us aspire to return to that state in which we were so removed from a particular language that all languages were ours. To put it another way, we are all the impossible translators of dreams, for dreams speak within us what no word is capable of saying.

Our purpose, as producers of dreams, is to gain access to that other language no one can speak, that hidden language in which all things can have all names. What the sick woman was asking was what we all wish for: to annul time and send death to sleep.

Maybe you expected me, coming as I do from Africa, to use this platform to lament, to accuse others, while absolving my immediate fellows from guilt. But I prefer to talk about something of which we are all victims and of which we are all guilty at the same time: how the process that has impoverished my continent is in fact devitalizing our common, universal position as creators of stories.

In a conference that celebrates the value of words, the theme of my talk is the way dominant criteria are devaluing good literature in the name of easy and immediate profitability. I am talking about a commercialism that is closed to other cultures, other languages, other ways of thinking. The words of today are increasingly those that are shorn of any poetic dimension, that do not convey to us any utopian vision of a different world.

What has ensured human survival is not just our intelligence but our capacity to produce diversity. This diversity is nowadays being denied us by a system that makes choices solely on the grounds of profit and easy success. Africans have become the "others" once again, those who have little to sell, and who can buy even less. African authors (and especially those who write in Portuguese) live on the periphery of the periphery, there where words have to struggle in order not to be silence.

My dear friends:

Languages serve to communicate. But they don't just "serve." They transcend that practical function. Languages cause us to be. And sometimes, just as in the story I mentioned, they cause us to stop being. We are born and we die inside speech; we are beholden to language even after we lose our bodies. Even those who were never born exist within us as the desire for a word and as a yearning for a silence.

Our lives are dominated by a reductive and utilitarian perception that converts languages into the business of linguists and their technical skills. Yet the languages we know— and even those we are not aware that we knew—are multiple and not always possible to grasp with the rationalist logic that governs our conscious minds. Something exists that escapes norms and codes. This elusive dimension is what fascinates me as a writer. What motivates me is the divine vocation of the word, which not only names but also invents and produces enchantment.

We are all bound by the collective codes with which we communicate in our everyday lives, but the writer seeks to convey things that are beyond everyday life. Never before has our world had at its disposal so many means of communication, yet our solitude has never been so extreme. Never before have we had so many highways, and yet never before have we visited each other so little.

I am a biologist and I travel a lot through my country's savannah. In these regions, I meet people who don't know how to read books. But they know how to read their world. In such a universe where other wisdoms prevail, I am the one who is illiterate. I don't know how to read signs in the soil, the trees, the animals. I can't read clouds and the likelihood of rain. I don't know how to talk to the dead, I've lost all contact with ancestors who give us our sense of the eternal. In these visits to the savannah, I learn sensitivities that help me to come out of myself and remove me from my certainties. In this type of territory, I don't just have dreams. I am dreamable.

Mozambique is a huge country, as huge as it is new. More than 25 languages are spoken within it. Ever since independence, which was achieved in 1975, Portuguese has been the official language. Forty years ago, only a tiny minority spoke this language, ironically borrowed from the colonizer in order to disaffirm the country's colonial past. Forty years ago, almost no Mozambicans had Portuguese as their mother tongue. Now, more than twelve percent of Mozambicans have Portuguese as their first language. And the great majority understands and speaks it, stamping standard Portuguese with the imprimatur of African cultures.

This tendency towards change places worlds that are not distinguished only by language, in confrontation with each other. Languages exist as part of much vaster cultural universes. There are those who fight to keep alive languages that are at risk of extinction. Such a fight is an utterly worthy one and recalls our own struggle as biologists to save animals and plants from disappearance. But languages can only be saved if the culture that harbours them can remain dynamic. In the same way, biological species can only be saved if their habitats and natural life patterns can be preserved.

Cultures survive for as long as they remain productive, as long as they are subject to change and can dialogue and mingle with other cultures. Languages and cultures do what living organisms do: they exchange genes and invent symbioses in response to the challenges of time and environment.

In Mozambique, we are living in an age when encounters and disencounters occur within a pot bubbling with exuberance and paradox. Words do not always serve as a bridge between these diverse worlds. For example, concepts that seem to us to be universal, such as Nature, Culture, and Society, are sometimes difficult to reconcile. There are often no words in local languages to express these ideas. Sometimes, the opposite is true: European languages do not possess expressions that may translate the values and concepts contained in Mozambican cultures.

I remember something that really happened to me. In 1989, I was doing research on the island of Inhaca when a team of United Nations technicians arrived there. They had come to carry out what is generally known as "environmental education." I don't want to comment here on how this concept of environmental education often conceals a type of messianic arrogance. The truth of the matter is that these scientists, brimming with good faith, had brought with them cases containing slide projectors and films. In a word, they had brought with them educational kits, in the naïve expectation that technology would prove the solution to problems of understanding and communication.

During the first meeting with the local population, some curious misunderstandings emerged that illustrate the difficulty of translating not so much words but thoughts. On the podium were the scientists who spoke in English, myself (who translated their words into Portuguese), and a fisherman who translated the Portuguese into the local language. It all began when the visitors introduced themselves (I should mention here that most of them happened to be Swedish). We are scientists, they said. But the word "scientist" doesn't exist in the local language. The term chosen by the translator was *inguetlha*, which means "witch doctor." In those folks' eyes, therefore, the visitors were white witch doctors. The Swedish leader of the delegation (unaware of the status conferred upon him) then announced: "We have come here to work on the environment." Now, in that culture, the idea of the environment has no autonomous meaning and there is no word that exactly describes such a concept. The translator hesitated and eventually chose the word *ntumbuluku*, which has various meanings, but refers above all to a sort of Big Bang, the moment when humanity was created. As you can imagine, these island folk were fascinated: their little island had been chosen to study a matter of the highest, most noble metaphysical importance.

During the course of the dialogue, the same Swedish member of the delegation asked his audience to identify the environmental problems that were of greatest concern to the islanders. The crowd looked at each other, perplexed: "Environmental problems?" After consulting among themselves, the people chose their greatest problem: the invasion of their plantations by the *tinguluve*, or bush pigs. The *tinguluve*, interestingly, are also believed to be the spirits of the dead who fell ill after they stopped living. Yet whether they were spirits or pigs, the foreign expert didn't understand very well what these *tinguluve* were. He had never seen such an animal. His audience explained: the pigs had appeared mysteriously on the island and had begun to multiply in the forest. Now, they were destroying the plantations.

"They're destroying the plantations? Well, that's easy: we can shoot them!"

The crowd's reaction was one of fearful silence. Shoot spirits? No one wanted to talk or listen anymore, no matter what the subject. And the meeting came to an abrupt end, damaged by a tacit loss of trust.

That night, a group of elders knocked on my door. They asked me to summon the foreigners so that they could better explain the problem of the pigs. The experts appeared, astonished by this interruption to their sleep.

"It's because of the wild pigs."

"What about the pigs?"

"It's because they're not quite pigs…"

"So what are they, then?" they asked, certain that a creature couldn't exist and at the same time not exist.

"They are almost pigs. But they're not complete pigs."

Their explanation was going from bad to worse. The pigs were defined in ever more vague terms: "convertible creatures," "temporary animals" or "visitors who had been sent by someone." Eventually, the zoologist, who was by now getting tired, took out his manual and showed them the photograph of a wild pig. The locals looked and exclaimed: "Yes, that's the one." The scientists smiled, satisfied, but their victory was shortlived, for one of the elders added: "Yes, this is the animal, but only at night time." I have few doubts that, by this time, the experts doubted my ability as a translator. In this way, they didn't need to question what they were saying, or query how they had arrived in an unknown locality.

Whatever the correct translation might be, the truth is that the relationship between the experts and the local community was never good and no manner of modern PowerPoint presentation could make up for the initial misunderstanding.

In some languages in Mozambique, there isn't a word for "poor." A poor person is designated by the term *chisiwana*, which means "orphan." In these cultures, a poor person isn't just someone who doesn't possess assets, but above all it is someone who has lost their network of family relationships, which, in rural society, is a support mechanism for survival. The individual is considered poor when he or she doesn't have relatives. Poverty is loneliness, a family rupture. It is possible that international experts, specialists in writing reports on destitution, don't take sufficient account of the dramatic impact of

Pensativities

destroyed family links or of social networks for mutual help. Whole nations are becoming "orphans," and begging seems to be the only route to torturous survival.

By recounting these episodes, I wish to reinforce what we already know: the systems of thought in rural Africa are not easily reduceable to European processes of logic. Some who seek to understand Africa plunge into analyses of political, social and cultural phenomena. To understand the diversity of Africa, however, we need to get to know systems of thought and religious universes that often don't even have a name. Such systems are curious because they are often rooted in actually negating the gods they invoke. For most of the peasantry in my country, the issues surrounding the origin of the world just don't exist: the universe quite simply has always existed. What is the role of God in a world that never had a beginning? This is why, in some religions in Mozambique, the gods are always referred to in the plural, and have the same names as living people. The problem with God, according to a Makua proverb, is the same as that of the egg: if we don't hold it properly we drop it; if we hold it too hard, we break it.

In the same way, the idea of the "environment" presupposes that we humans are at the centre and things dwell in our orbit. In reality, things don't revolve around us, but we, along with them, form one same world; people and things dwell within one indivisible body. This diversity of thought suggests that it may be necessary to storm one last bastion of racism, which is the arrogance of assuming that there is only one system of knowledge, and of being unable to accept philosophies that originate in impoverished nations.

I have been talking about the various cosmovisions found in rural areas of Mozambique, but I wouldn't want you to look at them as if they were essentialisms, resistant to time and the dynamics of exchange. Today, when I revisit the island of Inhaca, I see that campaigns have been mounted to kill the wild pigs that invade plantations. Local chiefs prepare for the visits of foreign scientists using their mobile phones. Throughout the country, millions of Mozambicans have appropriated the words "culture" and "nature" and have absorbed them into their cultural universes. These new words are working on top of the original cultures, in the same way that certain trees invent the ground out of which they appear to be growing.

In short, cultural phenomena aren't stopped in time, waiting for an anthropologist to turn up and record them as some proof of an exotic world, outside modernity. Africa has been subject to successive processes of essentialization and folklorization, and much of what is proclaimed "authentically African" is the result of inventions external to the continent. For decades, African writers had to undergo the so-called test of authenticity: their texts were required to translate that which was understood to be their true ethnicity. Nowadays, young African writers are freeing themselves from "Africanness." They are what they are without any need for proclamation. African writers seek to be as universal as any other writer in the world.

It is true that many writers in Africa face specific problems, but I prefer not to subscribe to the idea that Africa is a unique, singular and homogeneous place. There are as many Africas as there are writers and all of them are reinventing continents that lie inside their very selves. It is true that a high proportion of African writers face challenges in order to adjust their work to different languages and cultures. But this is not a problem that is exclusively ours, those of us who are African. There isn't a writer in the world who doesn't have to seek out his or her own identity among multiple and elusive identities. In every continent, each person is a nation made up of different nations.

One of these nations lives submerged and is made secondary by the universe of writing: this hidden nation is called orality. Yet orality is not a typically African phenomenon, nor is it a characteristic that is exclusive to those who are erroneously called "native peoples." Orality is universal territory, rich in thoughts and sensibilities that can be reclaimed by poetry.

The idea persists that only African writers suffer what is called the drama of language. It is true that colonization induced traumas over identity and alienation. But the truth, my friends, is that no writer has at his disposal a language with its norms all tidy. We all have to find our own language in order to demonstrate our uniqueness and unrepeatability.

The Indian sociologist, André Beteille, once commented: "having one language makes us human, being at home in more than one is what makes us civilized." If this is true, Africans—assumed down the ages to be uncivilized—may be better suited to modernity than even they themselves think. A high proportion of Africans know more than one African language and, apart from these, speak a European language. That which is generally seen as problematic may after all represent considerable potential for the future. For this ability to be polyglot may provide us Africans with a passport to something that has become perilously rare nowadays: the ability to travel between different identities and to visit the intimacy of others.

Whatever the case, a civilized future implies sweeping and radical changes in this world that could be ever more our world. It implies the eradication of hunger, war and poverty. But it also implies a predisposition to deal with the material of dreams. And this has everything to do with the language that lulled the sick woman to sleep at the beginning of my talk. The man of the future should surely be a type of bilingual nation: a language with an organized set of norms, capable of dealing with visible, everyday matters, but one fluent, too, in another language to express that which belongs to the invisible, dreamlike order of existence.

What I am advocating is a plural man, equipped with a plural language. Alongside a language that makes us part of the world, there should be another that makes us leave it. On the one hand, a language that creates roots and a sense of place; on the other, a language that is a wing upon which to travel.

Alongside a language that gives us our sense of humanity, there should be another that can elevate us to the divine.

Keynote address to the WALTIC International
Literature Conference, Stockholm, Sweden, 2008.

THE SEVEN
DIRTY SHOES

I SHALL BEGIN by confessing to a certain uneasiness. While it is a pleasure and an honour for me to accept this invitation to be with you, at the same time, I don't know how to do justice to such a pompous title: "learned address." I have deliberately chosen a theme about which I have a certain amount of ill-contained ignorance. Every day, we are confronted by the rousing exhortation to fight poverty. And all of us, in response to our most generous, patriotic spirit, yearn to join this battle. There are, however, various types of poverty. And among all of these, there is one that escapes all manner of statistical and numerical indicators: this is the impoverishment of our ability to reflect upon ourselves. I speak of our difficulty in thinking of ourselves as the subject of history, as a place of departure from and destination for a dream.

I shall use the occasion in my capacity as a writer, having chosen the terrain of our inner being, a field in which we are all amateurs. In this domain, no one has a degree, nor can anyone be audacious enough to give "learned addresses." Our only secret—our only wisdom—is to be true to ourselves, and unafraid of publicly sharing our most vulnerable feelings.

That is what I have come here to do: to share with you some of my concerns, my solitary musings.

On my eleventh birthday, 5th July 1966, Kenneth Kaunda stood in front of the microphones of Radio Lusaka to announce that an essential pillar of his people's happiness had just been built. Kaunda thanked the Zambian people for their involvement in the creation of the country's first university. Some months before, Kaunda had launched an appeal for each Zambian to make a contribution to the construction of the university. The response was moving: tens of thousands of people answered the appeal. Peasants gave corn, fishermen donated fish, civil servants gave money. A country of illiterates drew together to create what they imagined would constitute a new page in their history. The message from the country folk at the university's official opening read as follows: *We gave because we believe that by so doing, our grandchildren will no longer feel hunger.*

Forty years on, the grandchildren of Zambian peasants still suffer from hunger. In fact, Zambians today are worse off than they were at that time. In the 1960s, Zambia benefited from a Gross National Product comparable to Singapore and Malaysia. Nowadays, there is no possible comparison between our neighbour and those two Asian countries.

Some African nations can justify their ongoing poverty because they went through wars. But Zambia never had a war. Some countries can argue that they don't possess any natural resources. But Zambia is a nation with considerable mineral resources. Where does the fault lie for these frustrated expectations? Who failed? Was it the university? Was it society? Was it the whole world that failed? And why did Singapore and Malaysia progress while Zambia regressed?

I spoke at random of Zambia as an African country. Sadly, there is no shortage of other examples. Our continent is full of identical cases, of failed targets and frustrated aspirations. We suffer from a general lack of belief in our ability to change the destiny of our continent. It's worth asking ourselves: what is happening? What needs to change both within and outside Africa?

These are serious questions. We cannot delude ourselves in our answers, nor continue to create a smokescreen in order to conceal responsibilities. We cannot accept that responsibility is merely the concern of governments.

Fortunately, our situation in Mozambique is unique and clearly distinct; we must acknowledge and be proud of the fact that our trajectory has been very different. One of these differences has only recently emerged. Ever since 1957, only 6 out of 153 African heads of state have abandoned power of their own volition. Joaquim Chissano is the seventh of these presidents. This may seem like a detail, but it is indicative that the political process in Mozambique has been guided by a different line of thinking.

Nevertheless, the conquests of freedom and democracy we enjoy today will only become definitive when they are transformed into culture within each one of us. And this will take generations to achieve. In the meantime, Mozambique lives under the same threats that are common to the whole continent. Hunger, poverty, disease, all this we share with the rest of Africa. The statistics are frightening: ninety million Africans will die from AIDS in the next twenty years. Mozambique's contribution to this tragic figure will be about three million dead. Most of those who are doomed are young and represent precisely the lever with which we could remove the weight of poverty. What I mean is that Africa isn't just losing its present, but it is losing the cornerstone upon which another future might be built.

It costs a lot of money to have a future. But it is far more expensive if all you have is a past. Before Independence, there was no future for the Zambian peasants. Now, the only time that exists for them is the future of others.

Are the challenges greater than our hopes? Our only course of action is to be optimists and do what the Brazilians call getting up, shaking the dust off, and starting again. Pessimism is a luxury reserved for the rich.

Ladies and gentlemen:

The crucial question is this: What is it that stands between us and the future we all want? Some believe that we lack more experts, more schools, more hospitals. Others believe we need more investors, more economic projects. All of this is necessary, all of this is vital. But for me, there is something else that is even more important. This thing has a name: it's called a new attitude. If we don't change our attitude, we won't gain a better quality of life. We can have more technicians, more hospitals, and more schools, but we won't be the builders of our own future.

I speak of a new attitude, but the word should really be uttered in the plural, because it contains a vast array of postures, beliefs, ideas and prejudices. For a long time now, I have defended the notion that the biggest factor in Mozambique's backwardness isn't found in its economy, but in our inability to generate a way of thinking that is productive, audacious and innovative. Thinking that doesn't come from the repetition of clichés, of formulas, or of prescriptions that have been invented by others.

I sometimes ask myself: why do we find it so difficult to think of ourselves as the subjects of History? It comes, above all, from having always inherited from others the contours of our own identity. At first, Africans were invalidated. Their territory was one of absence, their time outside History. Later, Africans were studied as if they constituted some clinical case. Now, they are helped to survive in the backyard of History.

We are all at the beginning of an internal struggle to overcome our ghosts of old. We cannot enter modernity with the burden of prejudices that we currently bear; we need to shed our footwear at the door of modernity. I have counted seven dirty shoes that we need to leave at the threshold of this new era. There are many more. But I had to choose and seven is a magical number.

The First Shoe: The Idea that the Guilty Are Always Others and that We Are Always the Victims

We are already familiar with this type of discourse. Blame has been attributed to the war, colonialism, imperialism, apartheid: in a word, to everything. Except ourselves. This washing of our hands has been encouraged by some African elites who seek to remain immune from liability. The guilty are pinpointed right from the start: they are the others, people of a different ethnic group, a different race, or from some other geographical area. It is true that others have had their share of responsibility in our suffering. But some of that responsibility was always homegrown.

Some time ago, I was struck by a book entitled *Capitalist Nigger: The Road to Success*, by a Nigerian called Chika A. Onyeani. In one of our newspapers, I reproduced a text by this economist, which is an impassioned appeal for Africans to regard themselves in a new way. Allow me to read you an excerpt from the text.

> *Dear Brothers:*
> *I am utterly tired of people who only think of one thing: to complain and lament as part of a ritual in which we present ourselves psychologically as victims. We weep and moan, we moan and weep. We complain* ad nauseam *about what others have done and continue to do to us. And we think the world owes us something. I am sorry to have to tell you that this is no more than an*

*illusion. No one owes us anything. No one is disposed to
abdicate from what they have, with the justification that
we also want the same thing. If we want something then
we must learn how to get it. We cannot go on begging,
my brothers and sisters.*

*Forty years after Independence we still blame the
colonial masters for everything that happens in Africa
today. Our leaders are not always honest enough to
accept responsibility for the poverty of our peoples. We
accuse the Europeans of stealing and pillaging Africa's
natural resources. But I ask you this: who is inviting the
Europeans to behave in this way? Is it not we?*

We want others to treat us with dignity and without
condescension. But at the same time, we continue to treat
ourselves with a kind of benevolent complacency: we are
experts in the creation of a discourse that absolves us from
any guilt. And so we say:

> someone steals, poor soul, because he is impoverished
> (forgetting that there are thousands of other impover-
> ished people who don't steal);

> officials and the police are corrupt because, poor things,
> their wages aren't enough (forgetting that no one in this
> world has enough wages);

> politicians abuse their power because, poor things, these
> practices are anthropologically legitimate in so-called
> traditional Africa.

Abdication from any responsibility is one of the most
serious stigmas that weighs upon us Africans, from North to
South. There are those who claim that it is an inheritance of
slavery, of that time when we were not masters of our fate. The
boss, often far away and invisible, was responsible for our destiny. Or for our absence of any destiny.

Today, we haven't even killed off the boss of former times
symbolically. One of the modes of address that has emerged

most rapidly over the last ten years is the word "boss." It was as if he had never really died, as if he were waiting surreptitiously for a historic opportunity to reappear in our daily lives. Can we blame anyone for this re-emergence? No. But we are creating a society that produces inequalities and that reproduces power relationships we believed were dead and buried.

The Second Shoe:
The Idea that Success Is Not Born from Work

Only today I woke up to the news of an African president who is going to have his three-hundred-room palace exorcized because he hears "strange" noises during the night. The palace is so out of proportion to the wealth of the country that it took twenty years to complete. It's possible president's sleepless nights are not so much the product of evil spirits but the product of a guilty conscience.

Either way, this episode merely illustrates the way we still explain, by and large, positive and negative phenomena. That which explains misfortune sits side by side with that which justifies being blessed. The sports team wins, the work of art is awarded a prize, the company is in profit, the official got promotion? To what is all this due? The first answer, my friends, is one we are all familiar with. Success is due to good luck. And the term "good luck" means two things: we are protected by our dead ancestors, and we are protected by our living godfathers.

Success is never, or almost never, seen as the result of effort, or of work as a long-term investment. Our experiences (good or bad) are attributed to invisible forces that command our destiny. For some, this causal view is seen as so intrinsically "African" that we would forfeit our "identity" if we abdicated from it. Debates about "authentic" identities are always treacherous; what we should be debating is whether we can create a stronger, more productive vision that encourages a stronger, more active, and more participatory approach to History.

Sadly, we see ourselves more as consumers than producers. The thought that Africa might produce art, science and ideas is alien even to many Africans. So far, the continent has produced natural resources and a labour force. It has produced footballers, dancers, craftsmen. All this is acceptable because it belongs to the realm of what people understand as "nature." But few will accept that Africans can be producers of ideas, of ethical positions, of modernity. It isn't necessary for others to repudiate this possibility. We ourselves assume the burden of such repudiation.

According to a proverb, "the goat eats wherever he's tethered." All of us are familiar with the sorry use of this saying and how it governs the actions of people who take advantage of situations and of places. It's sad enough that we compare ourselves to a goat. But it's also symptomatic that, in these proverbs of convenience, we never identify ourselves as animals that are producers, such as, for example, the ant. Let us imagine that the saying has changed and became the following: "A goat produces wherever he's tethered." I'll bet that in this event, no one would want to be a goat.

The Third Shoe: The Prejudiced View That Whoever Criticizes Is an Enemy

Many people believe that with the end of the one-party state, intolerance towards those who thought differently would come to an end. But intolerance isn't just the fruit of political regimes. It is the product of cultures and religions, it is the result of History. We have inherited a notion of loyalty from rural society that is too parochial. This failure to encourage a critical spirit is still more serious when it concerns our youth. The rural world is based on the authority of age. The young man, who has not married and produced children, has no rights at all, no voice and no visibility. The same process of marginalization oppresses women as well.

This whole legacy doesn't help create a culture of honest, open debate. Personal aggression is therefore largely substituted for the discussion of ideas. It's enough to demonize everyone who has a different opinion. There is a whole range of demons at people's disposal: political colouring, spiritual colour, skin colour, social origin or religion.

In discussing this matter, there is a historical component that we must consider: Mozambique was born out of a guerrilla struggle. This legacy imbued us with an epic sense of History and a deep sense of pride in the manner in which independence was won. But, through inertia, the armed struggle for national liberation also gave way to the idea that the people were a kind of army which could be commanded through military discipline. In the years following independence, we were all militants, we all had only one cause, our entire souls kowtowed in the presence of our leaders. And there were so many leaders. This legacy didn't encourage the capacity for positive insubordination.

At this point, I'm going to let you into a secret: in the early 1980s, I was one of a group of writers and musicians who were given the responsibility of producing a new national anthem and a new party anthem for FRELIMO. The way in which this task was received is indicative of our military discipline: we were given our mission, we were requisitioned from our jobs, and at the orders of the president, Samora Machel, we were shut away in a house in Matola, having been told that we would only be allowed to leave when we had completed the anthems. This relationship between power and the artists only makes sense within a given historical moment. The truth was that we accepted the responsibility with dignity, the task was presented to us as an honour and a patriotic duty. And in fact, once there, we more or less behaved ourselves. It was a time of great privation . . . and the temptations were many. In the house out in Matola, there was food, there were servants, a swimming pool, at a time when the city was suffering all kinds of shortages. During the first few days, I have to confess, we were fascinated by such privileged treatment and we allowed ourselves to while away the hours in idleness. This adolescent feeling of disobedience was our way of reaping small-scale revenge on regimental discipline.

The words of one of the hymns reflected this militaristic attitude, this metaphorical approximation that I have been referring to:

We are soldiers of the people
Marching forward

All this has to be seen in its context, without any rancour. In the end, this was how *Beloved Fatherland* saw the light of day: an anthem which sings of us as one people, united by a common dream.

The Fourth Shoe:
The Idea that by Changing the Words, Reality Changes

One of our countrymen was once giving a presentation on our economic situation in New York, and at a certain point he spoke of the black market. It was as if the end of the world had arrived. Angry voices were raised in protest, and my poor friend had to stop, without really understanding what was happening. The following day, we received a small dictionary of terms that were deemed politically incorrect. Terms such as blind, deaf, fat, thin, and so on, were banished from the language.

We have been pulled along by these cosmetic preoccupations. We are reproducing a discourse that privileges the superficial and suggests that by changing the icing, the cake becomes edible. Nowadays, for example, we hear people hesitating over whether we should say "negro" or "black." As if the problem lay in the words themselves. The strange thing is that, while we amuse ourselves discussing this choice of words, we still go on using terms that are openly derogatory, such as "mulatto" and *monhê* (although the etymology of this latter word isn't immediately insulting).

There is a whole generation that is learning a language—the language of *workshops*. It is a simple code, a kind of creole half way between English and Portuguese. In fact, it's not a language but a vocabulary package. It's enough to know how to manipulate one or two fashionable terms in order to talk to others (that is, to not say anything at all.) I strongly recommend some of these terms, such as for example:

sustainable development;
awareness or accountability;
good governance;
capacity building;
local communities.

These terms should preferably be used in a PowerPoint presentation. Another secret to cut a good figure in workshops is to be able to use abbreviations, for a "workshopper" who is worth his salt knows these codes inside out. Let me cite a possible sentence from a hypothetical report: *the MGDs from UNDP equated themselves with NEPAD from the AU and with PARPA from the GoM.* For those in the know, half an acronym is more than enough.

I'm from a time when our worth was measured by what we did. Today, what we are is measured by the spectacle we make of ourselves, by the manner in which we place ourselves in the shop window. The resumé, the business card (full of titles and flourishes), the list of publications that almost no one has read, all this seems to suggest one thing: appearances now have greater value than our capacity for action.

Many of the institutions that ought to be producing ideas are now producing reports, which clutter up shelves and are doomed to a useless archive. Instead of solutions, problems are found. Instead of action, new studies are recommended.

The Fifth Shoe:
The Shame of Being Poor and the Cult of Appearances

The hurry to show one isn't poor is, itself, proof of poverty. Our poverty cannot be a reason for hiding it. The one who should be ashamed isn't the poor person but the person who creates poverty.

Nowadays, we experience an obsessive concern with exhibiting false signs of wealth. The idea has been born that the status of a citizen derives from the signs that distinguish someone from those who are the poorest.

I remember that I once decided to buy a new car in Maputo. When the salesman saw the car I had chosen, he almost had a fit. "That one, Mr Couto? Surely, sir, you need a vehicle that is compatible." It is a curious term: "compatible." Compatible with what? I ask you.

Our lives are a stage performance: a vehicle is no longer an object with a function. It is a passport to a status of importance, the source of vanity. The car has become a reason for idolatry, a kind of temple, a true obsession in our self-promotion.

This illness, this religion that one might call "cardolatry," has afflicted everyone, from government leaders to street kids. Boys who can't read may well know the makes and details of all manner of cars. It's sad that their horizon of ambitions should be so empty and limited.

Our schools urgently need to exalt humility and simplicity as positive values. Arrogance and exhibitionism are not, as some would have it, expressions of some inherent African power culture. They are the expressions of those who accept packaging over contents.

The Sixth Shoe: Passivity in the Face of Injustice

We are predisposed to denounce injustice when it is committed against ourselves, our group, or those of the same ethnicity or religion as ourselves. We are less willing when the injustice is directed against the "others," or furthermore, when perpetrated within silent zones of injustice, these areas in Mozambique where crime remains invisible. I refer in particular to the following:

> domestic violence (40 percent of crimes are the result of domestic aggression towards women);
> violence against widows;
> violence against or maltreatment of workers
> violence against or maltreatment of children.

We were deeply shocked by the recent advertisement which stated that white candidates were preferred for jobs. Immediate measures were taken and this was absolutely correct. However, there are opportunities for discrimination that are just as serious or even more so, and that we accept as natural and beyond question.

Let us take that advertisement in a newspaper and imagine that it was worded correctly instead of racially. Would everything have been all right? I don't know whether you are all aware of the print run of the *Notícias* newspaper. It has a print run of 13,000. Even if we assume that each copy is read by five people, we have to accept that the number of readers amounts to fewer than the residents of a district of Maputo. It is within this world that sales discounts and access to opportunities are shared. I mentioned the print run but left aside the problem are shared. Why are the messages of our newspapers restricted in their geographical circulation? How much of Mozambique is left outside?

It's true that this discrimination isn't comparable to the racist advertisement because it's not the result of an explicit, self-conscious act. But the effects of discrimination and exclusion from these social practices must be a cause for reflection and cannot be classified as normal. This "district" of 65,000 people who have access to information is today a nation within a nation, a nation that gets pride of place, that exchanges favours among its members, that lives in Portuguese, and sleeps with its head on the pillow of the printed word.

Another example. We are administering antiretroviral drugs to around thirty thousand patients with AIDS. This number may rise over the coming years to fifty thousand. This means that about 1,450,000 patients are excluded from treatment. This decision has terrible ethical implications. How are decisions made and who makes such decisions? Is it acceptable, I ask, that the lives of one-and-a-half million citizens should lie in the hands of a tiny group of medical scientists?

The Seventh Shoe: The Idea that in Order to Be Modern We Need to Imitate Others

Every day, we receive strange visitors in our home. They enter via the magic box called television. They create a relationship of virtual familiarity with us. Gradually, it's we who begin to believe we're living outside, dancing in the arms of Janet Jackson. Videos and the television industry not only tell us to buy, but they issue a whole other invitation: "be like us." This appeal to imitation falls upon us like a gift from heaven: the shame we feel at being ourselves becomes a springboard, an excuse for us to don this other mask.

Our cultural production has begun to parrot the culture of others. The future of our music may be a kind of tropical hip-hop; the fate of our cuisine may be McDonald's.

We talk of soil erosion and deforestation, but the erosion of our culture is even more worrying. The low esteem given to Mozambican languages (including even the Portuguese language) as well as the insistence that our identity is based in folklore, are both ways of whispering the following message in our ear: we'll only be modern if we become American.

Our society's history is similar to that of an individual. Both are marked by rituals of transition: birth, the end of adolescence, marriage, the end of life. I look at our urban society and ask myself: do we really want to be different? For I see Mozambique's rites of passage are faithfully reproducing colonial society. We are doing a waltz, in formal dress, at a graduates' ball that is identical to those of my youth. We are copying the end-of-course rituals based on models from medieval England. We get married in veils and garlands and we dump, far from the Avenida Julius Nyerere, anything that might suggest a ceremony more rooted in our land or in Mozambican tradition.

Ladies and Gentlemen:

I spoke of the burden from which we must free ourselves in order to enter modernity in both mind and body. But modernity isn't just a door made by others. We are also carpenters in its construction, and we should only be interested in participating in a modernity that we are also helping to build.

My message is a simple one: more than a technically skilled generation, what we need is a generation that is able to question technical matters. Youths that are capable of thinking anew about our country and the world. More than people prepared to give answers, what we need is an ability to ask questions. Mozambique doesn't just need to move forward. It needs to discover its own way forward in a fog-shrouded time and in a world that has no direction. Other people's compasses are of no use to us, other people's maps are of no help. We need to invent our own compass points. What we require is a past that isn't crippled with prejudice; what we need is a future that doesn't come to us disguised as financial prescription.

The university should be a centre for debate, a factory for active citizenship, a forge for fashioning social concerns and constructive rebellion. We cannot train young professionals to be successful in an ocean of misery. The university cannot agree to reproduce injustice and inequality. We are dealing with young people and with what should be youthful, fertile and productive thought. Such thought cannot be ordered, it isn't born out of nothing. It is born out of debate, innovative research, and an information system that is open and sensitive to what might best come out of Africa and the world.

The question is this: we talk a lot *about* young people. We don't talk much *with* young people. Or rather, we talk with them when they become a problem. Youth experiences this ambiguous situation, dancing between a romantic vision of themselves (as the life blood of the Nation) and a malign condition, a nest of dangers and concerns (AIDS, drugs, unemployment).

Ladies and Gentlemen:

It wasn't just Zambia that saw in education what a shipwrecked sailor sees in a lifeboat. We also deposited all our dreams in this need.

In a public meeting held last year in Maputo, an elderly nationalist said, with candour and courage, what many of us already knew. He confessed that he, along with many others who, in the 1960s, fled to FRELIMO, weren't just motivated by their dedication to the cause of independence. They risked their lives and crossed the frontier of their own fears in order to be able to study. The fascination with education, and a notion that education provides a passport to a better life, was present even in a world where almost no one could study. Restrictions were common throughout Africa. Up until 1940, the number of Africans attending secondary school was less than eleven thousand. Today, the situation has improved and this number has multiplied a thousandfold. The continent has invested in the creation of new skills. And this investment has undoubtedly produced important results.

However, it has gradually become obvious that more skilled technicians don't in themselves solve the problem of poverty in a nation. If a country doesn't possess strategies to produce solutions at the deepest level, then all this investment won't produce the desired effect. If the abilities of a nation are directed towards the enrichment of a tiny elite, then yet more skilled technicians will be of little value.

School is a means for us to aspire to what we don't have. Later, life teaches us to have what we don't want. Between school and life, what we need is to be honest and confess to those who are younger than us the things we don't know; that we, as teachers and parents are also seeking answers.

With the new government, the fight for self-esteem has re-emerged as a priority. This is correct and opportune. We must like ourselves, we must believe in our capabilities. But this appeal to personal pride cannot be based on empty vanity, on a kind of baseless futile narcissism. Some believe that we shall regain our pride by visiting the past. It's true that we need to feel we have roots and that these roots honour us. But self-esteem cannot be constructed merely out of materials from the past.

In fact, there's only one way to give ourselves due value: that is through our endeavours, through the work we are capable of carrying out. We need to know how to accept our condition without shame or complexes: we are poor. Or rather, we have been impoverished by History. But we were part of this History, and we were also impoverished by ourselves. The causes of our current and future failures also lie within us.

But the strength to overcome our historical condition also dwells within us. We shall know, just as we knew before, how to reconquer the certainty that we are producers of our own destiny. We shall have ever-greater pride in being who we are: Mozambicans constructing a time and a place where we are born every single day.

This is why it is worth agreeing to shed not only the seven shoes, but all the shoes that delay our collective march forward. For there is only one truth: it's better to advance barefoot than it is to stumble along in the shoes of others.

Address to the Higher Institute for Science
and Technology (ISCTEM), Maputo, 2006.

DREAMING
OF HOME

I COME FROM AFAR and I bring you what I believe is a shared message from my writer colleagues in Angola, Mozambique, Cape Verde, Guinea-Bissau and São Tomé & Príncipe. The message is the following: among us, Jorge Amado wasn't just the most widely read of foreign writers. He was the writer who had the greatest influence upon the birth of literature in those African countries where Portuguese is spoken.

Our literary debt to Brazil goes back centuries, to the time when Gregório de Matos and Tomáz Gonzaga helped create the first literary nuclei in Angola and Mozambique. But these levels of influence were restricted and bear no comparison with the deep and lasting impressions left by the author from Bahia.

It should be said (by way of a secondary confession) that Jorge Amado did more for the projection of Brazil as a nation than all the country's diplomatic institutions together. It's not a question of improving the work of such institutions, but of acknowledging the huge power that literature has. In this room, there are others who have also contributed to the grandeur of Brazil and built bridges with the rest of the world. I am speaking, of course, of Chico Buarque and Caetano Veloso.

To Chico and Caetano go our heartfelt thanks for the light and inspiration we find in their music and in their poetry. And to Alberto da Costa e Silva, our gratitude for his magnificent study of the historical reality of our continent.

During the 1950s, 60s and 70s, Jorge Amado's books crossed the Atlantic and had a huge impact on our collective imagination.

It must be said that the Bahian writer didn't travel alone: along with him came Manuel Bandeira, Lins do Rego, Jorge de Lima, Érico Veríssimo, Rachel de Queiroz, Drummond de Andrade, João Cabral de Melo Neto, and so many others.

In my house, my father—who was and is a poet—named one of his sons Jorge, and another one Amado. I was the only one to escape such a reference. I remember that in my family, passion for Brazil was shared between Graciliano Ramos and Jorge Amado. But there was no conflict: Graciliano revealed the bare bones and stones of the Brazilian nation, while Amado exalted the flesh and spirit of joy of that same Brazil.

In this brief statement, I would like to consider the following question: why this absolute fascination for Jorge Amado, why this immediate and lasting identification?

I should now like to go on and talk about some of the reasons for our love of Amado.

Clearly, the first reason is a literary one, and resides wholly in the quality of the Bahian writer's texts.

I happen to think that a writer's worst enemy can often be literature itself. Worse than not writing a book, is overwriting it. Jorge Amado knew the precise dosage to give his literature, and apart from the text itself, he knew how to remain an excellent storyteller and a notable creator of characters. I recall Adélia Prado's astonishment when, after publishing her first book of poetry, she confessed: "I wrote a book, and my God, I didn't lose the poetry." Jorge too wrote without ever ceasing to be a poet of the novel. This was one of the secrets of his fascination: the natural quality of his creativity, his elaborate spontaneity.

Today, when I reread his books, the intimate tone of his conversation stands out: it's a conversation in the shade of a veranda that begins in Salvador da Bahia and extends all the way across the Atlantic. In his fluid, relaxed narrative, Jorge writes away, and his characters leap from the page into our daily lives.

The Cape Verdean writer Gabriel Mariano wrote the following: "For me, the discovery of Amado was a revelation because I would read his books and I was in my own country. And when I came across Quincas Wateryell, I could see him on the island of São Vicente, on my street, the Rua de Passá Sabe . . ."

This existential familiarity was certainly one of the reasons for the fascination we felt for his work in our own countries. His characters were our neighbours, not in place, but in our lives. Poor folk, folk with the same names as ourselves, folk with the same racial backgrounds as ourselves, paraded through the Brazilian author's pages. There were our own loafers, the temples where we spoke with our gods, the aroma of our food, the sensuality and the perfume of our women. Deep down, Jorge Amado made us return to ourselves.

In Angola, the poet Mário António and the singer Ruy Mingas composed a song, the words of which go like this:

When I read Jubiabá
I believed I was Antônio Balduíno
My Cousin, who never read it
Was Zeca Camarão.

And so this was the feeling: António Balduíno was already living in Maputo and Luanda before being given life as a literary character. The same happened with Vadinho, Guma, Pedro Bala, Tieta, Dona Flor and Gabriela, and with so many other incredible characters.

Jorge didn't write books, he wrote a country. And it wasn't just an author who reached us: it was Brazil in its entirety returning to Africa. So there was another distant nation, but one that wasn't foreign to us. And we needed this Brazil like people who need a dream they have never known how to have before. It might have been a stereotyped, idealized Brazil, but it was a magical space where we could be reborn as creators of stories and producers of happiness.

We discovered this nation at a historical moment when we had no nation. Brazil—so full of Africa, so full of our language and our religious spirituality—gave us a shore that we lacked in order to become a river.

I have spoken of literary and almost-ontological reasons that help explain why Jorge is so loved in African countries. But there are other, possibly more circumstantial reasons.

We were living in a colonial dictatorship. The works of Jorge Amado were banned. Bookshops were closed and publishers persecuted for distributing his works. Our encounter with our Brazilian brother therefore had a taste of adventure in its affront to authority and its clandestine nature. The circumstances in which we shared his subterranean aspirations to freedom also contributed to the mystique of the author and his writing. The Angolan writer José Luandino Vieira, who was sentenced to fourteen years' imprisonment in the Tarrafal concentration camp, passed a letter through the bars of his cell in 1964 in which he made the following request: "Send my manuscript to Jorge Amado to see if he can get it published over there in Brazil."

In fact the nationalist poets of Mozambique and Angola raised Amado like a flag. There's a poem by our own Noémia de Sousa called "João's Poem," written in 1949, which begins like this:

> João was young like us
> João had clever eyes,
> His hands held out,
> His head directed towards tomorrow,

João loved books that had soul and flesh
João loved the poetry of Jorge Amado

There is one last reason, which we could call a linguistic one: on the other side of the world, the possibility of another side to our language was being revealed.

At the time, we needed a Portuguese without Portugal, a language that while belonging to the Other, could help us find our own identity. Until we found Brazilian Portuguese, we spoke a language that didn't speak to us. And having a language like that, merely half a language, is another way of remaining speechless. Jorge Amado and the Brazilians gave us back our speech, in another Portuguese, sweeter, more rhythmic, more in our style.

The greatest Mozambican poet, José Craveirinha, had this to say in an interview: "I should have been born in Brazil. For Brazil had such an influence on me that as a child, I even played football with Fausto, Léonidas da Silva, Pelé. But we were forced to go through João de Deus, D. Dinis, the classics from Portugal. But at a certain point, we broke free with the help of the Brazilians. And all our literature became a reflection of Brazilian literature. When Jorge Amado reached us, we had found our way home."

Craveirinha was speaking of that great gift which was our ability to dream of home. That's what Jorge Amado gave us. And that's what made Amado ours, an African, and made us Brazilian too. For having turned Brazil into a home made for dreaming, for having turned his life into an infinite number of lives, we are grateful to you, Jorge, our companion.

Speech on Jorge Amado, São Paulo, Brazil, 2008.

TRAVELLING
FIRE RAISERS

ONE of the debates to which I have been invited to contribute in Mozambique is aimed at combatting the so-called "uncontrolled bush fires." This fight seems totally justified: it is about protecting ecosystems and conserving useful and productive spaces.

However, I fear it may be one of those thankless battles that has no chance of immediate success. In reality, we do not understand the complex ecology of fire on the African savannah. We do not understand the factors that foreshadow fire. Despite this, I'm frequently asked to speak to the country folk about the noxious effects of rural fires. I have to confess that I've never been capable of fulfilling this task.

Instead I have tried to discover why country dwellers convert their grasslands into flames. We know that slash-and-burn agriculture is one of the main reasons for such fire-raising practices. But people don't often talk of that other guilty party, a character I shall call the "male visitor," and whom I shall talk about during the course of this brief address.

In the rural families of Mozambique, the division of tasks reveals a society in which most of the work falls on women's shoulders. Those who love nothing better than to quantify social relations have already published figures and tables that provide abundant proof that while the man rests, the woman is busy all day long. But this same peasant is involved in other things that escape the notice of social accountants. Among the invisible occupations carried out by the rural man, the most obvious is that of visitation. This activity is central to the rural societies of Mozambique.

The man spends months of the year visiting neighbours and distant relatives. These visits do not appear to have a practical or well-defined purpose. When one asks one of these visitors what the purpose of his journey is, he replies: "I'm just visiting." In fact, visiting is a way of preventing conflicts and creating harmonious relations that are vital in a society that is dispersed and lacking in the state mechanisms that guarantee stability.

Visitors spend much of their time in rituals of welcome and leave-taking. To open the doors of a place requires an understanding with the ancestors that are the place's true "custodians." These male visitors therefore cover incredible distances on foot. As they progress, they set fire to the grass. Unless it's in the middle of winter, the grass doesn't burn much. The fire spreads and peters out in the immediate vicinity of the paths taken by our travellers. These fires have a number of purposes and advantages that become clear on the return journey: they provide a reference map, discourage snakes and the dangers of ambush, provide a firm footing and altogether make the return journey easier and safer.

As an intruder in this form of logic, I have never accepted the militancy with which I have been expected to combat these fires: nor have I ever been able to convince one of these travelling fire raisers to desist from his activity. And it's absolutely true that I'm not sufficiently moved by conviction. Even if I had strong beliefs on the subject, I would never be able to convince any of these country dwellers to do otherwise. For they are motivated by reasons that are not solely practical. We shall come back to these reasons later on.

The question that provides the excuse for our meeting here is a simple one: what causes us to wander when we could stay quietly where we are? This question induces other ones. Some of them are near to my domain of knowledge: is the desire to travel written into our genes? Is it part of our nature?

I believe that the essential characteristic of Mankind is to have no essential character. That's why, when we ask ourselves about Man's predilection for walking, the answers should be sought in our history. It's here that we shall understand the origin and development of this preference. It's here that we shall understand our time-honoured appetite for travel.

Our species was nomadic for hundreds of thousands of years. If we accept that our birth as a subspecies dates from 250,000 years ago, we have had 12,000 years of sedentary existence as opposed to 240,000 years as nomads. Almost 90 percent of our existence has therefore been spent as hunters, wandering across the African savannah.

During the entire childhood and adolescence of our species, our primary vocation was hunting. Hence our constant, intrinsic need to leave, search, turn our space into a territory for gathering and for hunting our prey. Our link to a place was always provisional, ephemeral, lasting for as long as the seasons and the bounty lasted. We had no idea of how to take possession. And perhaps we didn't know how to take possession of the soil because we were scared of being possessed by it. We survived because we were eternal wanderers, hunters of chance, visitors in places that were yet to be born.

Hunting isn't limited to the act of ambush and capture. It suggests that we can read signs in the landscape, listen to different types of silence, master languages and share codes. It suggests that we learn through play, just as feline animals do; it suggests that we develop a taste for fear and fright, and it suggests that we gain skill in the art of surprise and in the game of pretence. We produce our prey, but, above all, it was our prey that made us into a creative, imaginative species. For thousands of years, we perfected a culture of exploiting our environment; we had an inquisitive relationship with our surroundings. For millennia, our home was a world without a fixed dwelling place.

That is why it is puzzling that we should ask ourselves nowadays why we like to wander so much. The theme of our meeting should, in fact, be inverted. Why have we developed a taste for standing still? To stay behind is the exception. Leaving is the rule. *Homo sapiens* survived because he never ceased to travel. He spread over the planet, he left his footprint beyond the last horizon. And even when he remained behind, he was always leaving for places he discovered within himself.

With the birth of agriculture, we developed a sense of place. From then on, we started giving names to places, we tamed the ground. Ties of kinship between humanity and the landscape were forged. The earth took on the quality of the divine; it became a mother. For the first time, we had roots, we lived in an endless season. The ground didn't just provide us with a bed. It was a womb. And it required an enduring marriage.

Paradoxically, sedentary life ushered in the idea of exile. The appetite for travelling now needed to be limited. Sowing was what was now required. The land now became an object of possession. The idea of a frontier became inscribed as a tacitly accepted law. Beyond, lay the realms of others. The world began to have an "inside" and an "outside," an "over here" and an "over there." And so travelling began to bring with it additional risks. Fear began to grow that one might never return. The first epic journey in literature—the story of Ulysses—is the narrative of a return. The exaltation of return atoned for the fear of departure.

It's possible that this may have been the case. It's impossible to know for sure. Maybe this distinction in time periods is too arbitrary, too literary. Perhaps things were more complex, more mixed. We are all the mestizo descendants of hunters, gatherers and sowers of seed.

What is important is that our relationship with travel has never been objective, cold, or exempt from fantasy. Even the hunters of old, those who lived as travellers, even they carried out rituals in order to familiarize themselves with the unknown. Before reaching their destination, they sent their collective imagination on ahead. Just as they painted the animals they were going to hunt on the walls of their caves, they fantasized over distant places; they dressed them in beliefs and turned them into narratives. In the end, even when we lived in caves, we had travel agents who domesticated the unexpected for us, while stimulating our taste for adventure.

And so that's what happened: both the remotest desert and the most impenetrable forest were peopled with our ghosts. That's why all places nowadays begin with a name, a legend, a myth, stories. There is no such thing as an external geography as far as we are concerned. Places—no matter how unknown to us—reach us dressed with our own imagination. The world no longer lives outside a map, and it doesn't live outside our own inner cartography.

I shall now return to the male visitor, that fire raiser of the Mozambican prairies, in order to get to know his hidden reasons better. None of them ever paid me any attention and I almost take pride in my failure. Our travelling fire raiser must be imagined in a world where the highway is a luxury and transport a rarity.

This is the reality of the savannah that I am obliged to travel in my work as a biologist. And I have to confess that I experience a fearful shudder when the outline of a path is no longer visible in front of me. Love of wandering seems to collide with the absence of a road. Faced with a world with no footprints, I am assaulted by an eerie sense of fragility, as if I had committed some religious offence, a disrespect for a law dating from before the arrival of men. In such circumstances, I also feel like lighting a thread of fire myself in order to give distance a human dimension.

Apart from the practical simplicity of the phenomenon, the truth is that the travelling fire raiser is a map-maker and is recording the signs of his presence on the landscape. He writes the narrative of his journey with fire. Not because he is scared of getting lost, but because he wants geography to come and drink from his hand. The travelling fire raiser says: "I am the master of fire. My gesture makes and unmakes landscapes. There is no horizon where I may get lost, for I am a creator of paths. I am master of fire and I am master of this world that I cause to burn. My kingdom is one of smoke and ash. At the moment when my flames consume everything, at that moment alone, am I divine."

When it comes down to it, we are like this visitor. The difference is that in our case, it's not the landscape that burns, but we ourselves. We become consumed in that moment when, even as we stand still, we set off in search of what we cannot be. We are recreating the world, refashioning it in the manner of one of our childhood books. We are playing with our fate like the cat who pretends the ball of wool is a mouse.

In the beginning, we travelled because we read and listened, propelling ourselves forward in boats made of paper, on wings made from ancient voices. Today, we travel in order to be written, to be words in a text that is greater than our own Life.

Address to the Conference on Travel Literature,
Matosinhos, Portugal, 2006.

THE PLANET
OF FRAYED SOCKS

O VER the last few days, I had been struggling against time in order to assemble this speech, until a colleague, noticing my difficulties, made the following suggestion: "You've already given an address called 'The Seven Dirty Shoes.' Why don't you write another one now called 'The Seven Frayed Socks'?"

It wasn't more than a passing joke, but when I got home, I came across an extraordinary photo of the President of the World Bank, Paul Wolfowitz. In it the man is shoeless, at the entrance to a mosque in Turkey, and clearly visible are his toes peeping out from his frayed socks. The photo was flashed around the world and, who knows, given its subject, the showy uniform may well become *de rigueur* among the financiers and bankers of our planet.

Whatever the case, there was an uncanny coincidence between my colleague's joke and the photo in the magazine, and I ended up calling this text "The Planet of Frayed Socks." The magazine which featured the photo wanted to portray the absurd side of Wolfowitz's situation. As far as I was concerned, however, being caught like that merely made one of the most powerful men in the world a more familiar, more human creature.

What I mean is that the shoe may be very different, but the big toe poking through the banker's sock is very similar to the toe of the poorest Mozambican. Just like any of us, the President of the World Bank conceals blemishes beneath his composed appearance.

I was told that the theme of this lecture was free, but at the same time, it was suggested that I should talk about the Human Person. Socks in need of darning can, suddenly, show us up to be more human, and make us ever more like those who appear distant.

So I shall start by telling you of an episode that I have never recounted before and whose revelation here may prove costly to me. Who knows: having shared this secret with you, I may find my accounts frozen or that I've been permanently designated a *persona non grata* in the world of Mozambican finance.

It happened right after Independence. I was about to set off on an overseas trip, and at that time, there weren't the facilities we enjoy nowadays. The most a traveller could have at his disposal was a so-called traveller's cheque. To get traveller's cheques was a fearfully complicated process, and it was almost necessary to direct one's request to the President of the Republic. I was travelling for urgent health reasons and two hours before boarding the plane, I was still in the bank, desperately trying to get my wretched cheques. At that moment, a lethargic bank teller informed me somewhat tragically that the cheques would, in fact, require two signatures, mine and my wife's. Now, my wife was at work and there was no time to get the cheques to her. In the depths of my despair, there was only one thing for it. I was going to have to lie. I told the bank teller that my wife was outside in the car, and that I would bring him everything duly signed in less than a minute.

I took the cheques outside and hurriedly forged my part-ner's signature. I did this under a considerable amount of nervous pressure, and without her original to copy from. The signature looked awful, smudged, and patently false. I rushed back inside, gave him back the papers and stood there wait-ing. The man retreated into an office, took his time, and then re-emerged with a solemn expression to tell me: "I'm sorry but there's a signature here that doesn't match." I was expecting this, but even so, I crumbled under the weight of my shame. "I'd better tell him the truth," I thought to myself. And I'd already begun to speak, "The problem is, comrade, that my wife . . . ," when he interrupted to make this alarming declaration: "Your wife's signature is fine, but your signature doesn't match!"

As you can imagine, I was speechless and spent the next few moments practising my own signature in front of the sus-picious gaze of the bank teller. The harder I tried, the less I was able to imitate my own handwriting. During those end-less minutes, I thought to myself: "I'm going to be arrested not for having forged someone else's signature. I'm going to be arrested for forging my own."

I tell this story because the theme suggested for my address is the human person. At that time, as I stood in front of those ill-fated traveller's cheques, I underwent the strange experi-ence of someone caught red-handed being himself.

The truth is that we are never just one, but various peo-ple, and it should be the norm that our signature never quite matches. We all live alongside various selves; a variety of people all claim our identity. The secret is to disallow those choices life imposes, which kill our inner diversity. The best thing in life is to be able to choose, but the saddest thing is actually having to choose.

My dear friends,

Words dwell so deep within us that we forget they have a history. It's worth asking ourselves about the word "person," and that is what I shall do as simply and straightforwardly as possible. The word "person" comes from the Latin *persona*. This term is associated with masks and theatre. *Persona* was the space between the mask and the face, the space where the voice gained tone and vibrancy. In its origin, the word "person" referred to an empty space filled with imitations, just as I, in the episode of the traveller's cheques, was imitating someone else. Today we are not so far removed from its original meaning, in which we don masks in the performance of the narrative that we call "our life."

In the languages of southern Africa, the word "person" is in a particularly interesting category. A German linguist noted in the nineteenth century that many languages of Sub-Saharan Africa used the same word for "person": *muntu* in the singular, and *bantu* in the plural. He called these languages "Bantu" and, by extension, the people became "Bantu people." This is strange because he seemed to be saying, quite literally, that this group was called "the people people." I remember an *mbira* player, a Cameroonian called Francis Bebey, whom I met in Denmark. I asked him if he played Bantu music and he laughed at me and replied: "My friend, the Chinese are as Bantu as we Africans."

In any case, the idea of a person has a different origin in Africa, and has evolved differently from the European concept, which is now global. In African philosophy, each person exists because he or she is all the others, and this collective identity is arrived at through the family.

We are like a Makonde sculpture of the extended family; we are a branch of that huge tree that gives us body as well as shade. In contrast to the norm nowadays in Europe, we view modern society as a network of extended family relations. As we shall see, this vision has two sides to it: a positive side that makes us accepting and leads us towards that which is universal, and a parochial side that confines us to our home village. The idea of a world in which we are all relatives of one another is very poetic, but it is often not practicable.

We all know the attitude of the average Mozambican: the government is our father, and we are the children of those who are powerful. This family-based vision of the world can be dangerous, for it invites us to accept the social order as natural and immutable. Modernity is whispering something very different in our ear, which is forcing us to make a radical break with our own tradition. Unlike our parents, whom we can't choose, we can choose our leaders. The company or the institution don't consist of a group of cousins, uncles or brothers-in-law. The logic they follow in order to function is impersonal and is subject to criteria of efficiency and economic yield that have no time for ties of kinship. We can wear shoes with or without frayed socks. But it's hard to put one's socks on after one's shoes.

We have to think of ourselves as living in a world of rapid transformations. The speed of change in modern society has the effect of making some professions obsolete quickly. In Brazil, for example, computerization in the banking sector has reduced the number of jobs by 40 percent in the last seven years. This implies dramatic changes with serious impacts on society. We are on the crest of a wave of changes that are not limited to technology. Cellphones, for example, have stopped being merely utilitarian. Cellphones have become part of us, so much so that when we forget to take them with us, we feel empty, unarmed, as if we had left at home a limb we didn't know we had.

This subtle occupation extends beyond our private lives. Organized crime, for example, is now directed from inside prisons. News reports following the trial of those responsible for killing the journalist Carlos Cardoso shows us what others already knew: a prisoner isn't the one behind bars, a prisoner is the one who doesn't have a cellphone.

Even distance is no longer measured in terms of kilometres. We want to know whether there is cell reception where we are going. The end of the world is where one's phone stops working.

It's true that the new technologies don't stitch holes in our underwear, but they do alter the social networks with which we make our lives. In many African languages, the word for "poor" is the same as for "orphan." Being poor is losing one's family networks and web of social alliances. The person who has lost the support of the family lives in poverty. In the very near future, the true orphan will be the person who doesn't have a computer, a cellphone, or a credit card.

We live in a society that glorifies the individual but denies the person. It seems like a contradiction, but it isn't. There is, after all, some distance between these two terms: an individual and a person. An individual is an anonymous, faceless being, without any existential contours. The history of each one of us is that of an individual on a journey towards personhood. What makes us into people isn't our identity card; what makes us into people is that which doesn't fit on identity cards, is the way we think, the way we dream, the way we are others. So we are talking here about citizenship, about the possibility of being unique and singular, about our ability to be happy.

One of the problems of our age is that we have lost the capacity to ask important questions. School taught us just to give answers, and life advises us to keep quiet. A question that may be important is this one: what hinders our transition from individuals to people? What do we need in order to be fully integrated persons?

I won't assume that my answers are the right ones. But I get the feeling that one of the main problems, one of the biggest holes in our sock is thinking that success isn't the fruit of work. For us, success, in whatever field, comes as a result of what we call "good luck." It comes from having good patrons. Success comes from who one knows rather than what one knows.

This week one of the editions of the newspaper *Notícias* opened with an item on Monte Tumbine, in the province of Zambezia. In 1998, about one hundred people died there as a result of a landslip. There was a landslide because the forest on its slopes had been cut down, and the rains caused the earth to slip. Reports were written and their recommendations were very clear. The reports vanished. The forest went on being cut down and people once again settled in dangerous areas. What remains in Monte Tumbine are the voices, which have another explanation. These voices insist on the following version of events: there's a dragon that lives in Milange, on Monte Tumbine, and it awakens every five years to go and lay its eggs out at sea. In order not to be seen, the dragon creates chaos and darkness while it crosses the skies unnoticed. This mythological animal is called Napolo in the north, while here in the south, it goes by the name of Wamulambo.

This interpretation of geological phenomena contains a powerful, poetic force. But poetry and spirit ceremonies are not enough to guarantee that another tragedy won't be repeated.

My question is this: We here in this meeting, are we so removed from such beliefs? The fact that we live in cities, surrounded by computers and broadband internet connections, does all this exempt us from having one foot in a magical explanation of the world?

All we have to do is take a look at our newspapers to get an answer. Next to the international exchange rates, we find the advertisement of a so-called traditional doctor, that generous character who offers to solve all the basic problems in our lives. If you look down the list of services offered by traditional doctors, you will see that they include the following (I shall omit the miracle cures they produce):

> making you get on in life;
> helping you gain promotion in your job;
> making you pass your exams;
> helping you get your husband or wife back.

Parodying the jargon used in reports nowadays, I would say that this is a fair "job description" for our magnificent traditional doctor. This purveyor of fortune invokes, through his magic, all those things that can only be achieved through sweat, effort, and hard work.

Once again, we must question the words that we ourselves create and use. "Traditional doctors" is a doubly false term. Firstly, they are not doctors. Medicine is a very specific domain within the field of scientific knowledge. There are no traditional doctors, just as there are no traditional engineers or traditional airline pilots.

It's not a question of denying the value of local wisdom, nor of devaluing the importance of rural logic. But these self-advertisers aren't doctors and they are not even "traditional." The practices of witchcraft are profoundly modern: they are being born and refashioned right now in our urban centres. A good example of this ability to incorporate the modern is that of an advertisement I kept from a newspaper, in which one of these quack healers described his services textually as follows: "We cure asthma, diabetes and pimples; we provide treatment for sexual diseases and headaches; we eliminate misfortune and . . . we make photocopies."

For a long time, real doctors were not permitted to publicize their services in the press. And yet these other so-called traditional ones are still allowed to advertise. What is the reason for such complacency? Because, deep down, we are predisposed to believe them. We belong to this universe even as we simultaneously imagine the world in other ways. It's not just the poor, the less educated who share these two worlds. There are university educated officials, political leaders who seek their blessing in order to get promoted or to be successful in their careers.

I don't believe it is enough to condemn such practices; but we must admit them more openly. Returning to the title of this talk, we must accept that within the shoe, our feet require a very special form of ventilation. It's of little use to say these things are typically African. My friends, these things exist throughout the world. They are not part of the so-called exotic nature of Africans. They belong to human nature.

We can say, however, that these beliefs still have a decisive influence, and this influence contradicts some of the exigencies of modern life. Belief in so-called "good luck" makes us shun our individual and collective responsibility: such a vision of the world attributes our failures to a supposedly hidden hand. If we fail, it's because someone turned the evil eye on us. We don't assume the role of active, responsible citizens. We don't produce our own destiny: we beg from powerful forces that are beyond us. We wait for a blessing or a stroke of good fortune. This is a central problem in our development.

The belief in "luck" is one facet of a more all-embracing and sophisticated conspiracy theory; we explain everything via plots hatched behind our backs. It is the fear of witchcraft brought into the sphere of political analysis. The recent case of timber is a good example of the application of this conspiracy theory. A group of our countrymen denounced acrtions it thought were going to lead to the imminent destruction of our forest patrimony. It was a serious warning: we could lose not only part of our natural environment, but one of the main weapons to fight against poverty. The reaction against this protest wasn't long in coming: various articles all asserted that this concern for our forests came from a well-intentioned group of people, who were manipulated by Western forces busy mobilizing against the Chinese presence in Africa. Here is the dark hand that commands everything.

As in the logic of witchcraft, the identification of the wrongdoer immediately solves the problem. Once the smoke-screen has been created and the finger pointed in accusation, the matter of the forests will lose its visibility. The question here is simple: wouldn't it be easier to create a scientific commission to record the current state of our forest resources and to assess the real implications of timber extraction? It is too important a matter, my friends, for us to pretend we have dealt with the protester's concerns merely because we raise the suspicion of an international conspiracy. The truth is that if we lose our forest, we lose one of the greatest reserves of our wealth, and the biggest living resource in the whole of our country.

Dear friends,

Our belief in good or bad luck is something that stifles our ability to show enterprise, something that consolidates within us a spirit of victimhood. To improve our world, we are constantly invited to think our only options involve begging, lamenting, or complaining. I shall let you into another secret. The firm I work for placed an advertisement for young people to carry out surveys in different parts of Maputo. Hundreds of young people applied and it seemed certain that the two dozen candidates whose applications were successful would cling to their jobs tooth and nail.

However, on the first day, half a dozen of them presented complaints: they couldn't work in the sun, the work was very tiring and they needed more breaks, they needed a subsidy in order to buy hats and sunshades . . . This, my friends, is the spirit of a nation that's sick. A country in which young people put in their requests before they've even given anything, is a country that may have mortgaged its future.

The point I wish to make is that, along with a limitless capacity for self-denial, we still suffer from the delusion that we deserve more than others because we suffered in the past. "History is in debt to us," this is what we think. But History is in debt to everyone and doesn't pay anyone back. All peoples have suffered terrible mistreatment and damage at some point. Whole nations have been reduced to rubble and have been re-born through the efforts and toil of generations. Our own country was able to escape the conflagration of war. Invoking the past in order that people may pity us, and then awaiting compensation, invited only illusion.

This positioning of ourselves as victims to whom the world must pay a debt occurs at both the national level and that of individual citizens. As we have survived personally on favours, we ask the world to concede us privileges and special dispensations. The plain truth is this: we shall never be accorded such privileges. Either we conquer them for ourselves or we shall never get them. The value of Lurdes Mutola derives from the fact that she overcame a whole background of difficulties. Let us imagine that Lurdes Mutola, instead of training hard, were to insist on being able to start the race a few metres ahead of her rivals, arguing that she was poor and came from a country that had suffered hardship. Even if she won, her victory would have no value. The example might seem ridiculous but it highlights the kind of self-pity that we have displayed countless times. The solution for the underprivileged isn't to ask for favours. It is to fight harder than others, and above all to fight for a world in which favours are no longer needed.

Another hole in our socks (this hole is as big as the sock itself) is our tendency to blame others for our own mistakes. If we lose our job, it's not because we haven't turned up for work repeatedly without any justification. If we lose our girl-friend (or boyfriend), it's not because we've loved them little and badly. We fail an exam, but it's never because we've failed to prepare adequately for it. We explain these slip-ups by evoking demons, the existence of which we find deeply comforting. The fabrication of devils is, after all, a long-term investment: our conscience can sleep easily, sheltered by such illusions.

This isn't an illness that is exclusive to us. Nowadays, we witness dramatic examples of this tendency to fabricate ghosts: every day, in Iraq, innocent civilians are killed in the name of God, in the name of the struggle against the devil, incarnated in others, of other beliefs. It was José Saramago who said, "Killing in the name of God makes that God an assassin."

And now let us return to the matter of human beings. Throughout history, aggression against others always begins, curiously, by depersonalizing them. The first US operation against Vietnam was not of a military character. It was psychological in character and consisted in dehumanizing the Vietnamese. They were no longer humans: they were "yellow," they were beings of another type, upon whom one could drop bombs, Agent Orange and napalm without ethical problem.

The genocide in Rwanda occurred not so far from here and not that long ago. Communities that lived in harmony were manipulated by criminal elites to the point of committing the biggest massacre in contemporary history. If we asked a Tutsi or a Hutu before 1994 if they believed such a thing could happen in their country, they would have answered that it was impossible to imagine. But it happened. And it happened because the capacity for creating demons in our countries is still considerable. The poorer a country is, the greater its capacity for self-destruction.

Beginning in April 1994 and for the next one hundred days, more than 800,000 Tutsis were murdered by their Hutu fellow countrymen. Axes and knives were used to butcher 10,000 people every day, which works out at an average of ten people every minute. Never before in human history had so many been killed in such a short time. All this violence was made possible because once again, efforts had been made to prove that the others were not human beings. The term used by Hutu propaganda to describe the Tutsis was "cockroaches." The massacre was thus exempt from any moral objection: it was insects being killed, not people, and certainly not compatriots speaking the same language and living the same culture.

In neighbouring Zimbabwe, the discourse of unity that characterized the beginnings of a multiracial society was suddenly altered to take on a markedly racist and aggressive tone. The vice-president of Zimbabwe, at a political rally in Bulawayo, stated openly that "whites aren't human beings." He was merely repeating what Robert Mugabe had proclaimed. And at this point, let me cite Mugabe: "What we hate about whites isn't their skin but the devil that emanates from them." The leaders of ZANU had distinguished themselves only a few years before as defenders of a multiracial nation. What had changed? It was the forces at play. Ambition for power provokes surprising changes in people and political parties.

In Mozambique, such dark clouds, we know, are remote and unlikely to ever happen here. This is reason for pride and faith in the future. But this certainty requires us to remember the lessons of a history that is ours as well.

Dear friends,

I was asked to talk about people. This subject is a vast, limitless universe in which no one can claim to be a specialist. I was forced to choose just a tiny corner of this boundless canvas. I spoke of the evil that is our abdication from responsibilities, our abandonment of our capabilities. I spoke of our dependency on a way of life in which everything is obtained through favours, through contacts and handouts. I spoke about all this because the banking system is profoundly vulnerable and permeable to these situations.

The real question that we have to face as a nation concerns our ability to produce more wealth, but we mustn't confuse wealth with easy money. I once gave an address on our obsession with getting rich quickly no matter how. I was the target of demagogic claims that I didn't want to see rich Mozambicans. I shall finish today by reiterating that which I have always defended:

My desire is not only to see rich Mozambicans in the true meaning of the word "rich." My desire is to see all Mozambicans sharing this same wealth. Only this will make us more human, more worthy of being called people.

Opening address to the
International Bank of Mozambique Millennium Conference,
Maputo, 2008.

HALF A FUTURE

I REMEMBER an experience I had as a journalist in 1974, during what we then called "the period of transition." We didn't know that it was only the first of an endless series of transition periods, and I sincerely hope that many more transitions will occur as we continue the process of discovery to which we have dedicated ourselves.

It was 7 April, 1975, the first time all Mozambique had commemorated the Day of the Mozambican Woman. I was working for the *Tribuna* newspaper, and was sent to cover the celebrations in the port of Maputo. The person in charge of the rally was our late and fondly remembered general, Sebastião Mabote.

Right at the beginning of the meeting, there were songs and the obligatory slogans were shouted, as was the custom in those days. The enthusiasm of the dockworkers was unrestricted, and their support for the speaker total. Mabote shouted "Long Live Women!" And hundreds of manly arms and harsh voices were raised in vigorous and unanimous accompaniment.

Suddenly the general paused, and from his improvised podium, contemplated the crowd, which consisted solely of men, hardened and muscular by the nature of their work. His look was one of a commander of souls, used to leadership. It was then that he issued his order: "Everyone shout with me. I want your voices to be heard far beyond Maputo." And the men answered as one that yes, they would join their leader in chorus. Then Sebastião Marcos Mabote raised his arms to encourage the masses, and launched forth with the following rallying cry: "We are all women! We are all women!" And he urged them, vigorously, to repeat his words. There was a shocked silence, and a wave of unease swept over the dock-workers. Some, just a few, timidly began to repeat the strange slogan. Mabote knew the art of communicating with the masses. And he persisted patiently until after some painful minutes, more and more masculine voices proclaimed their feminine identity. But no one did so wholeheartedly. And those who timidly raised their voices were never more than a tiny minority. This time, the general wasn't fully successful.

I share this memory with you because it confirms what we all know: it is easy (although it is becoming less common) to show one's solidarity with others. It's difficult to be the others. Not even if it's only for a fleeting moment, not even if it's just a brief visit. The dockworkers were disposed to declare their solidarity with women. But they weren't willing to travel over to their feminine side. And they refused to think of themselves as reborn beneath a different skin, within another gender. We say we are tolerant towards differences. But being tolerant is still not enough. We need to accept that most differences are invented and that the Other (the other gender, the other race, the other ethnic group) always exists within us.

It's obvious that I'm not talking literally about being the Other, I'm not proposing that we men become transvestites, parroting women's traits, painting our lips and nails, wearing bras and high heels. For men use this kind of disguise far more often than they would willingly admit. Let us not forget that during Carnival, the most common costume involves a man dressing up as a woman. It's almost an obsession. Even the most hardened males feel a strange compulsion to parade as women, on those days when it is socially accepted. It would be worth asking ourselves—even from a psychiatric point of view—why there is this desire to take on an identity that men otherwise repudiate so vehemently.

I'm not talking about this type of mimetic conversion. I'm talking about our willingness to travel over to what we understand as the soul of others: our capacity to visit, as ourselves, that which we might call the female soul, even if we don't quite know what that is, even if we do not know where the frontier between masculinity and femininity begins or ends.

I remember that at a conference on literature in Durban, a South African writer criticized one of his country's young poets. He said: "You wrote a verse about an African woman riding a bike in the country. But a Bantu woman would never do that." I had just come from a journey through Sofala and Zambezia and happened to have with me various photographs of women riding around on bicycles. I showed this proof of the crime, and the critic muttered bitterly: "Yes, but these aren't Zulu women." The world of the Bantus had suddenly and drastically been reduced to that of the Zulus. And it's quite likely that there were many Zulu women pedalling along the roads of South Africa without our friend being aware of it. But that's not the point. Even if no women from a given community use bicycles, literature is free to invent whatever it wants, and to place a female body—or that of a gender yet to be invented—in the saddle.

I think that the South African writer's reaction, born out of insecurity, reflects a male position that invokes supposed interdictions in the name of a hypothetical "female essence." It is the product of fear. We men do not know the women with whom we share our lives and the world. We fear what they are thinking, we feel threatened by what they feel. We view the future as if it were a bicycle being ridden by a woman. And so it was this profound, primal fear that came to the surface when the dockers had to shout the slogan proposed by Sebastião Mabote. Women may suffer the same challenge when being the Other and travelling through the souls of men, but something tells me they don't have the same fer of a male-dominated future: in fact they experience this now. The present is a pirate bus and a man is at the wheel.

It is against the deep-seated fear of otherness that Ibsen and all great writers worked. They were ahead of their times, constructing worlds beyond reality, and they enabled others to imagine because they had imagined themselves beyond the limits of their bodies and of what were generally accepted as their identities.

A hundred years later, we are celebrating the work of a man who represents a country, a language and a culture that are apparently so far removed from us. But we all become closer to each other in the struggle for humanity. Ibsen was a writer and a fighter. In the notes to his play, *The Doll's House*, he wrote: "A woman cannot be herself in this society that has been constructed as masculine, with laws drawn up by men and male judges who evaluate society on the basis of masculine criteria." And we Mozambicans view Mozambique as a male entity.

Our society is in a state of permanent and generalized violence towards women. This violence is silent (I would prefer to think of it as silenced) because of an extensive network of male kinship. Levels of domestic violence are huge, cases of rape are unacceptable, violence against widows has already been reported on in a book, and there is violence against elderly women who are accused of being witches and who are therefore punished and stigmatized. And there's more if we wish to illustrate the silent and systematic aggression against women: over 21 percent of women marry before they reach the age of fifteen (in some provinces, this number rises to nearly 60 percent). There are young girls who never get to be women. The cycle reproduces in such a way that a young girl who should still be a daughter is already the mother of a girl who, in turn will be impeded from exercising her femininity. Fifty-five percent of births by these young girls occur without the support of a qualified midwife. For all these reasons and many others, women between the ages of fifteen and twenty-four are twice as likely to be contaminated by AIDS as boys of the same age. These statistics suggest a process of silent mutilation in the country, a permanent state of war against ourselves.

This is the only conclusion we can draw: a country in which women can only be half themselves is condemned to live only half of its future.

Speech delivered at the commemoration
for the writer Henrik Ibsen, Maputo, 2007.

BARING
ONE'S VOICE

Two weeks ago, in this very place, Gilberto Mendes lamented the lack of culture among our elite. Gilberto complained about the politically media-conscious who only leave home to be present at gala performances of the National Song and Dance Company. They don't go to the theatre, they don't read books, they don't frequent cultural or artistic venues.

This systematic abstinence is sad, but I have to say that such absences don't only occur in our country. It's not a matter of the failure of any given government. We are facing an organized plan to fabricate "tradition" as the only genuine and truthful representation of national culture. By choosing "tradition" as the only yardstick of our identity, we are doing exactly what this event is supposed to be warning us against: we are killing culture. All culture thrives on its own diversity. Culture should always be spoken of in the plural.

People often talk of Mozambique as being a multicultural mosaic, but, deep down, they keep reminding us that the root of our Mozambican identity is this business of tradition. But this same tradition is very curious: on the one hand, no one seems able to define it exactly. On the other, it is in constant flux, and some things now seen as traditional were, in days gone by, acts of irreverence and audacity. The first women to wear *capulanas* in our country must have been viewed as provocative and disrespectful of traditional customs and morality. The same thing occurred with the *marrabenta*. And yet today, the capulana and the marrabenta have been incorporated as traditional emblems.

A young Mozambican sociologist by the name of Patrício Langa, wrote the following: "No one is more or less Mozambican because of the instrument he plays. We can all become Mozambican through what we do, and we can make what we do Mozambican. Music is no exception. No one could bear to live in a country where one only listened to the music of José Mucavele, no matter how Mozambican his music, or how morally and politically correct, how educated and ethnomusical, it is. I have a real phobia about the intentions behind those who present things as genuine or authentic. It was intentions like these that created Nazi ideologies, as well as people like Mobutu and his ideas of African authenticity. We don't want any more producers of murderous identities."

In fact, those in power find it very convenient to construct their official culture on the basis of tradition and folklore. In the name of this tradition, they can suddenly discover that democracy is not, after all, typically African. In the name of tradition, blind obedience can be justified and the distinction blurred between that which is the public patrimony and the private property of chiefs.

Young Mozambican city dwellers have a decisive role to play in shaking off this inertia, and furthermore in the production of new ideas and new forms of representation. What Patrício Langa is doing in sociology is something we hope other young people will do in their own fields. Many young people have done so, often with great courage, and while facing the type of harsh criticism and parochial envy that will resort to anything in order to stifle change.

Nowadays, we talk of globalization, and Mozambican hip hop (of which Dama do Bling is a well-known representative) is a good example of this phenomenon. In Mozambique, these currents began imitatively, but then took on Mozambican characteristics. People say this process is called globalization, but I must ask the assembly to excuse me from using the word, because it has become such a tired term that I have reached a state of irreversible saturation with regard to it. Globalization, sustainable development and other terms that it would be politically incorrect to name are expressions that have been uttered so often that they no longer mean anything at all.

We often complain that the youth of today subsist on a culture of imitation, but young people in the past did the same. This happens throughout the world, and has done throughout the ages. I also imitated and I think that almost everything begins when inspired by models from outside. My generation imitated the Beatles, the Rolling Stones, Elvis Presley, Otis Redding, Aretha Franklin. The best way to create one's own style is to absorb varied and diverse influences. One cannot, in the name of African purity (or any other invented purity), shut the door on other voices. Much of what we call "genuinely African" originated in the cultural exchange with other continents. Nowadays, this exchange is quicker and more effective than ever. But it has always existed: globalization began with the first man.

Through some strange inferiority complex, we are always afraid that others will come and influence us, and we never notice the reverse process. Today, the greatest writers in English are from Asia, the greatest fado singer is from Mozambique, and one of the greatest flamenco singers is a black woman from Equatorial Guinea. And even one of the most famous Portuguese bullfighters is called Ricardo Chibanga.

Certainly, rap and hip hop had their origin in Africa, and now they are returning, altered and Americanized. In the

United States, rap and hip hop were born out of political and social protest. Their words constituted, at the time, a radical criticism of serious social problems. The record industry greatly altered this irreverent character of rap. It kept the music, drained the words of any meaning, dressed up the artists, and replaced their social criticism with an extravagantly superficial stereotype. The aggressive and intimidating image of the street gangs became its defining characteristic. The celebration of violence and easy money became constant themes. Women became "bitches" and "hos" and men became "niggers" and "dogs." The poetry of the songs became degraded in their facile rhymes and in the way the genre's objectification of women and glorification of violence enforced a distorted view of young American blacks.

What became of the original rappers? In reality, some engaged voices still survive, as is the case of Lauryn Hill who, through her lyrics, continues to fight for social causes. But these cases no longer appear on TV. The new tribal rap of the gangs has gained complete hegemony, as if it were the only music young Americans produce. I don't watch much television, but I've never seen a clip showing the lives and struggles of poor Americans; I've never seen a clip showing the daily toil of those millions of workers who are building the American nation. Most video clips portray the easy life, with violent-looking young men at orgies surrounded by scantily clad girls, cavorting next to cars and by luxurious swimming pools, while they dance the whole time in a permanent display of hedonism.

I know that Dama do Bling has complained a lot about some of the criticisms that have been made of her. However, the authors of other types of music have extremely cogent reasons for feeling they are the victims of yet more discrimination. It's a fact that Dama do Bling has a major stake in a current that dominates the market completely and holds a monopoly of television viewers in thrall. It's very rare to see or hear other musical genres on television or radio. One can count on the fingers of one's hands the number of times voices such as that of Mingas, Wazimbo, Roberto Chitsonzo and others, are given any air time.

I began this talk by speaking about how certain elites make a point of pushing traditional music as the only valid form. The same restrictive and emasculating policy against diversity occurs on MTV, which seeks to reduce black American music to rap and hip hop. The same restrictive policy occurs on African radio stations, which give priority to so-called music for dancing, the music of DJs and the dance floor, over the great talents of our continent. How often does one get to see on television singers like Salif Keita, Ismaël Lô, Lokua Kanza, or Sally Nyolo? Are we not all the poorer because of this silent censorship?

And so I've mentioned the word censorship, because it can encourage appetites capable of really killing culture and killing José Craveirinha. There are those who might argue whether we should accept that there is censorship in our media. Well, let me tell you this: censorship exists. It exists and is practised against people who want to make other kinds of music. Those who don't have beautiful bodies, or aren't willing to swivel their hips in front of the cameras, risk being overlooked. Even if a musician is talented and has extraordinary vocal ability, he will be excluded.

In the cultural supplement of yesterday's *Notícias*, there was an entire article devoted to a dance spectacle, *Solo para Cinco*, in honour of Augusto Cuvilas. I haven't seen it, but apparently there is too much nudity in this dance show. The newspaper quotes three witnesses. The director of a cultural association has this to say: "This spectacle puts Mozambican cultural values in jeopardy." An artist has this to say: "I don't want to censor anything but whoever chose this play isn't one of ours. Mozambican culture will never veer towards nudity and people must accept our values." The third opinion is that of a political leader, who says: "This play is an attack on our cultural integrity . . . We aren't closed to the outside world, but in matters of culture we must be immovable."

We are faced with a sensitive issue, which we might term a prudish attitude. And in this matter, no matter which side we are on, we have to take care not to entrench positions and undermine the debate. I remember that immediately after Independence, I was arrested because I was walking along arm in arm with my wife. For the soldiers who detained me, what I was doing was immoral. Fortunately, nowadays young people can show their affection for one another without being disturbed. But in order not to be disturbed, we must be sure we aren't disturbing others. Gratuitous provocation can help justify those who defend ideas of censorship and repression.

We need time to absorb critically that which is new. We shouldn't be in a hurry in such matters. However, we can't put up with a morality that relies on hypocrisy, or which hurries to denounce feminine excess, but falls shy of denouncing male violence. Or one that hesitates in denouncing the rape of young girls and women, a domestic violence that causes much more harm than erotic dances on TV. The lyrics of Maboazuda are perhaps far more offensive than all the salacious dances of all the female rappers together.

The upholders of puritanism should remember the case of Zaida Chongo and recall the extraordinary popular demonstration that this singer's funeral became. There's a sign here, a warning that it is very dangerous to talk in name of an idealized culture. Imagine me going to see the paintings of Naguib, or Idasse, or Malangatana armed with this stupid prejudice against nudity. How many exhibitions of their paintings would the censors have to prohibit?

The idea that globalization brings immorality is very dangerous. Immorality doesn't come from outside. It already inhabits our society, it even inhabits that which others present as our tradition in all its purity. Globalization isn't required in order for our children to be raped. Globalization isn't required for domestic violence and aggression against women to occur.

In conclusion, we need to take the debate about music out of the realm of false morality, and refocus on the debate about artistic quality. What we need to know is whether Mozambican rappers are producing valid works of art, or just commercial products designed for success with audiences.

The artist, whether male or female, can dance and show off his or her body if this corresponds to some creative communication and is not a spectacle intended to show off a physique gratuitously. I would go further: a male or female artist may, in this context, turn nudity into an art form. However, the only thing expected of a singer is the baring of his or her voice.

Contribution to the debate "Don't Kill Culture,
Don't Kill Craveirinha," Maputo, 2008.

THE TANGLED
BALL OF WOOL

O NE of my earliest memories is this: I am sitting, my arms held out, in front of my mother, who gradually winds a ball of wool from a length of yarn hanging from my wrists. I was a child, but the task was more than a responsibility: I was giving life to an ancient ritual, as if, before me, there was another child from whose arms the same infinite ball of wool was being wound. This persistent memory that I savour, like an eternal patch of shade, almost serves as a metaphor for the work of memory: a delicate thread, joining other threads, being rolled up into a rounded belly.

I revisit that moment in my life by way of an introduction to the theme of this text. This is a meeting about memories and I begin with a recollection that establishes me as a producer of memories and other untruths. I shall return later to the ball of wool and the boundless peace of my childhood home.

We have been summoned here to talk of history and of memories, of peace and of wars. As if, as writers, we had a particular skill in such matters.

In a novel I'm currently writing, there's a character who is asked: "Where are you going to be buried?" To which he replies: "My final burying place doesn't dwell in the future. My grave is my past."

Each one risks entombment in our own past. It takes effort to avoid becoming imprisoned by memories, which are the simplified depictions of us that others have made. We all carry a book written in us, and this text seeks to impose itself as our source and as our destiny. And if there is a war within us all, it is a war of resistance, in which we refuse to be confined to a single and predictable narrative.

To speak of wars isn't a peaceful matter at all. And to speak of memories is a subject full of forgetfulness. It is strange to perceive a writer as someone who guards his past like a dockside watchman, someone who checks a ship's moorings. In fact, a writer is someone who unties the ship and invites us to set off on a journey. Every time he invokes the past, the writer is constructing a lie; he is inventing a time outside of Time. Liars who lie in order to be believed must be accorded a special mention in a debate like this.

Dear friends and colleagues, true colleagues in the craft of lying:

On the first day of this Congress, José Luís Cabaço asked why it is that our writers don't use the war of national liberation as a source of inspiration.

Fortunately, he raised this question on an earlier panel in which the topic was different; and the answer was postponed. If I had had to answer on that particular occasion, I would have said: because it's too near in time and because it's too near the dream. I would have said that the war was felt like a piece of fiction, that it was lived like an epic narrative. We are faced by a situation in which the character swallows the narrator, and the hero devours the author.

But his question was asked two days ago and, at home, I began to wonder whether there might be other reasons. I think there are. One such reason is this: the armed struggle for liberation has become removed from its previous affective proximity. The narrative of this historic process was gradually appropriated by a discourse of exaltation and became too grandiloquent. The epic lost its appeal; it was led by the heroes who gave their names to streets and squares, but have neither faces nor voices. We have inherited a heroic history of history-less heroes. Superhuman characters have ousted the common people, those humble folk who were scared, who hesitated, who fell in love, who became like all of us.

In truth, my friend Cabaço's question can be extended to other wars and other epic episodes in our country's history. Where are the histories of that History with a capital letter? They don't exist. Or maybe they exist in secret, remote hide-aways, but we may need to cross deserts to find them.

In fact, we haven't just forgotten our country's war of independence. We have forgotten the far more recent war of destabilization, the drama of which still echoes in our daily lives. We have forgotten the wars of colonial resistance, we have forgotten the wars of regional occupation (such as the one waged against the Nguni invaders), we have forgotten the wars of the *Prazeiros*, or land leaseholders, against the colonial authorities. And we have forgotten with proven efficacy, the never-ending war against slavery. This disremembering has a long history and is proof of our skill in the art of dismissing things from our mind.

Why are we so competent when it comes to forgetting, why are we so systematic in wiping away the footprints of time? The simplest answer lies in the absence of writing. In terms of temporal register, we are in no-man's land: oral witnesses have either never come forward or have been lost. This is certainly a major justification. But the absence of writing cannot explain everything. It can't explain, for instance, the alarming collective amnesia that has wiped away the external and internal signs of the recent civil war.

I believe we need to find other answers. It's not just the overwhelming power of orality that prevents us from recording deeds that caused us to be undone and then done up again. There must be another explanation for this strange need to exclude the past of our homegrown mythology. In the good old African way, we do not know how to transform our past into our prehistory.

I think this alternative explanation can be summed up as follows: we forget our wars because, in all these conflicts, we weren't all on the same side. We forget these conflicts because, in every one of them, we were scattered among the vanquished and the victors. We forget because at the time, we were not yet the entity we are today (Mozambicans, residents of the same existential home that is the Mozambican nation). These others that we once were find it hard to make the transition to what we "are" now. We were "them" and we keep ourselves in the third person in order to go on being "us," that collective entity born of wars, that people who have forgotten themselves. We don't know how to bury within us the part of us that gradually died. We don't have room in our soul for socially accredited memories, for those living cemeteries.

Let us start with the war of national liberation. When FRELIMO unleashed a general armed uprising, a call for mobilization was circulated that, at a certain point, went like this: *workers and peasants, labourers, intellectuals, officials, students, Mozambican soldiers in the Portuguese army, men, women...*

This particular reference to Mozambican soldiers in the Portuguese army deserves to be explained. There were up to 60,000 soldiers in the Portuguese colonial army. Of these, more than half were Mozambican. I am certain that, over the course of the ten-year war of national liberation, there were more Mozambicans fighting in the ranks of the colonial army than there were in the ranks of the nationalists. During the same period, tens of thousands of Mozambicans were not only in the regular colonial army, but also made up the bulk of the paramilitary forces such as the Flechas (Arrows), the Special Groups, the OPVDC (Provincial Organization of Volunteers and Civil Defence) and the Special Paratrooper Units. Not to mention the PIDE, or secret police. Let's not beat about the bush: we were on both sides in the war, we were victims and perpetrators, angels and demons.

But this distribution between paradise and the inferno didn't just occur in the war of national liberation. It occurred in the wars of resistance in which whole nations often allied themselves with the Portuguese in order to defend themselves from internal and external threats. Between the seventeenth and nineteenth centuries, the vast majority of the colonial troops consisted of black soldiers. The hero of anti-colonial resistance, Ngungunyane (so well portrayed in Ungulani Ba Ka Khosa's *Ualalapi*) was also a colonel in the Portuguese army. A Portuguese flag flew over his general headquarters. The deeds of many other potential resistance heroes (such as Farelay in Angoche), cannot be sung without risk of arousing the ghosts of those enslaved by them.

The same difficulty has exempted the long, dramatic period of slavery from any narrative record. Why do we have no memory of this tragedy? The answer may be this: it's because we were simultaneously slaves and slave traders.

To sum up, throughout our history, the victors and the vanquished have mingled and now, none of them wants to dis-inter times that are laden with guilt and resentment. Behind this demureness, there is an economy of peace, a mediation of silences, whose intelligence cannot be minimized.

The past is sacrosanct because it is the dwelling place of the dead. In order to gain access to this inner sanctum of respect, we need a founding myth that we can all agree to share. We lack this common "password" that may return time to us while also freeing us from remorse and the need to forgive and seek forgiveness. Our truth commission works because it is absent, and because in its haste to begin a new text, it only uses one key on the keyboard: the "delete" button.

It might be thought that the birth of the nation (through which we are still living) would be the most appropriate moment to assemble and reinvent our common heritage of memories. But exactly the opposite has occurred. This is our most fragile period, in which we are aware that we may be ambushed by the judgment of those who yearn for the past. This has happened in every country in the world: the beginning of a national narrative has been born out of what some have called "the syntax of forgetfulness." Processes of homogenizing agglutination suggest that different communities forget themselves, and different groups abdicate their singularities. We are one nation because we forget the same things in the same way.

We need to empty our memory of the symbolic territory of the nation in order to re-populate it, filling our imagination with new forms, in front of a mirror that reveals to us not so much what we are, but what we can be. In our haste to have a future, we cast aside the different stages of the journey we have completed. We have all experienced this recently. With the process of Independence, we forgot we had a race, a tribe, an individuality. Even if this sense of amnesia was false, the fact is that it was lived with the intensity of a truth.

I now return to the first episode I mentioned at the beginning of my talk, that memory of the way I wound woollen threads from my mother's hands. I do so in order to confess the following by way of conclusion: that moment, so full of peace and quiet, has another version. If you were to ask my mother, she would tell you it was hell. That's what she still tells me today: "You wouldn't keep still; you complained that it wasn't a boy's job, and I had to prod with my foot so we wouldn't end up with a ball of tangled wool."

This is the lesson: I have learned that if I want to celebrate my home, this home that after so many is my only home, I can't burden my mother with all my memories. One of us must forget. And both of us end up forgetting in order that the old home can be reborn from the shadows of time. In order that we don't entangle the ball of memory.

Address to the conference on Literature and the Memory of War, Mozambique Polytechnic University, Maputo, 2008.

WHAT IF OBAMA
WERE AFRICAN?

A FRICANS rejoiced in the victory of Obama. I was one of them. After a sleepless night, in the unreal half-light of early morning, my tears flowed as he delivered his victory speech. At that moment, I too had won a victory. The same happiness ran through me when Nelson Mandela was freed and elected as a new South African statesman, thus opening up a new route to the dignification of Africa.

On the night of 5th November, the new American president wasn't just a man who was speaking. It was the suffocated voice of hope re-emerging, liberated, within us. My heart had cast its vote, even without permission: not accustomed to asking for much, I celebrated a boundless victory. When I went out into the street, my city had relocated to Chicago, and blacks and whites were sharing their same joyous surprise. For Obama's victory wasn't that of one race over another: without the massive participation of Americans of all races (including that of the white majority), the United States of America would not have given us a reason to celebrate.

On the following days, I gradually gauged the joyous reactions from the most diverse corners of our continent. Anonymous people, ordinary citizens, wanted to register their happiness. At the same time, and with some reservations, I made a note of the messages of solidarity coming from African leaders. Almost all of them called Obama "our brother." And I thought: are all these leaders being honest? Could it be that Barack Obama is the relative of so many politically diverse folk? I have my doubts. In our haste to see prejudices only in others, we are unable to see our own racism and xenophobia. In our haste to condemn the West, we forget to take on board the lessons that reach us from that other side of the world.

It was then that I got hold of a text by the Cameroonian writer, Patrice Nganang, entitled: "What if Obama were Cameroonian?" The issues raised by my colleague from Cameroon suggested various questions to me, formulated around the following hypothesis: what if Obama were African and campaigning for the presidency of an African country? These are the questions I should like to explore in this text.

What if Obama Were African and Running for an African presidency?

1. If Obama were African, his rival (some African George Bush) would invent changes to the Constitution, enabling him to extend his mandate beyond that initially foreseen. And our Obama would have to wait a few more years before he could run again. He might have to wait a long time, if we take into account the period an African president can be in power: some 41 years in Gabon, 39 in Lybia, 28 in Zimbabwe, 28 in Equatorial Guinea, 28 in Angola, 27 in Egypt, 26 in Cameroon. The list goes on, including fifteen presidents who have governed for more than twenty consecutive years. Mugabe will be ninety years of age when he completes his mandate, which he imposed over and above the will of the people.

2. If Obama were African, it is likely that, as a candidate of the opposition, he wouldn't be given freedom to conduct a campaign. The same actions would be taken against him as occurred, for example, in Zimbabwe or Cameroon: he would be physically assaulted, he would then be arrested, and his passport would be confiscated. The George Bushes of Africa don't tolerate opponents or democracy.

3. If Obama were African, he wouldn't be an eligible candidate in most countries, because the elites in power have invented restrictive laws that close the doors of the presidency to the sons of foreigners and the descendants of immigrants. The Zambian nationalist, Kenneth Kaunda, is undergoing questioning in his own country because his parents were from Malawi. They conveniently "discovered" that the man who took Zambia to independence and governed the country for more than 25 years was, in fact, the son of Malawians, and had therefore governed "illegally" all that time. Arrested for an alleged plot to carry out a coup, our Kenneth Kaunda (who gave his name to one of the main avenues in Maputo) will be barred from political activity, just so the current regime will see itself free of an opponent.

4. Let us be clear: Obama is black in the United States. In Africa, he's a mulatto. If Obama were African, he would have his ethnic identity thrown in his face. Not because skin colour is important for people who expect their leaders to be competent and to work hard. But our predatory elites would mount a campaign against someone they would designate as "not truly African." The same black brother who is today greeted as the new American president would be vilified at home for being a representative of the "others," those of another race, of another flag (or of no flag at all?).

5. If our "brother" were African, he would have a lot of explaining to do to the local moralists when he included in his speech of thanks the support received from the homosexual community: a mortal sin for the proponents of so-called "African purity." For these moralists—so often in power, so often with power—homosexuality is an unacceptable vice that is foreign to Africa and to Africans.

6. *If* he won the elections, Obama would probably have to sit down and share power with his defeated opponent, in a degrading process of negotiation that proves in some African countries the sacrosanct—the will of the people expressed in the ballot box—can be eroded by the loser. At this stage, Barack Obama would be sitting at a table with some Bush or other, in the middle of endless rounds of discussion with African mediators, who are there to teach us that we should be satisfied with those crumbs of the electoral process that don't favour dictators.

Inconclusive conclusions

Let us be clear: there are exceptions to this generalized view of the situation. We all know what exceptions we are talking about and we Mozambicans were able to constitute one of them.

Let us also be clear: impediments to an African Obama would not be imposed by the people, but by those in power, by the elites who turn governing into a source of unscrupulous self-enrichment.

The truth of the matter is that Obama is not an African. It's true that Africans—the simple people and anonymous workers—celebrated Obama's American victory with all their hearts. But I don't think the dictators and corrupt leaders of

Africa have any right to an invitation to this celebration; the joy which millions of Africans felt on 5th November arose because they had invested in Obama precisely the opposite of what they have experienced with their own leaders. No matter how painful it is to admit this, only a minority of African states have had, or have, leaders concerned with the public good.

On the same day that Obama acknowledged his victory, the international news bulletins were packed with horrifying stories from Africa. Africa was still being crushed by wars, bad management, and the unbridled ambition of profit-seeking politicians. Having killed democracy, these leaders were killing politics. In some cases, war was still being waged. In others, hope had been abandoned and cynicism prevails.

There's only one real way to celebrate Obama in African countries: that is to fight so that more flags of hope may be unfurled in our continent. To fight so that African Obamas may win. So that we Africans, of all ethnic backgrounds and races, may win through these Obamas and celebrate in our own home that which we celebrate now in someone else's.

Article originally published in
Savana, Maputo, 2008.

NUTMEGGED
BY A VERSE

I N MY AREA of town, football was a reason for much celebration. We would get ready for the occasion, just as
believers get dressed for their saint's day. Sundays were a
time of mythical duration. And the field situated in an area
of waste ground in Muchatazina was a stadium that was bigger than the world itself. The game hadn't yet begun and our
hearts were already tired: there wasn't a clock big enough to
accommodate those ninety minutes.

It wasn't the hunger to win. I don't want to paraphrase
Pierre de Coubertin, but the important thing was to be there,
in that game of boundless performances that a football match
allows. Suddenly, the place we lived in migrated and our identity travelled to worlds where all was huge and aglow. This was
the great secret behind our beating hearts, behind this addic-
tion that made us run away from our homes, skip school,
leave our girlfriends waiting for us. When we were playing,
we ceased being ourselves. We ceased being. And we were
everything, everyone. The living and the dead were lined up
in the pantheon of those who never lost.

In my glorious team, I was the striker. It was, perhaps, a
euphemism to call me this, for all I did was dribble. I never

shot. My nickname in Chissena reflected this ability: I was *kiywa* , the dribbler. A "dribbleballer," as others teased me. On the other hand, I lacked a name for my inability.

"Hell! To win, you need to score, man! That guy's a poet. That's what he is: a poet."

That's what Joe Hotshot, our coach, said. Maybe coach was right. Maybe I wasn't really a forward. Maybe my field really was poetry. But the beauty of football isn't in the score. As in the art of love, the fascination lies in the preparations. The delight is in what can't be translated into a number or even a word. A football match is always worth more than the result. The most beautiful thing in a game is what can't be converted into goals and points; it's what eludes the radio commentator, it's the sighs and silences, the looks and the mute gestures of those playing both inside and outside the four straight lines of the pitch.

Let's go back to Hotshot. The frustration of the coach, in point of fact, had an explanation: in my hometown of Beira, the neighbourhoods were territories of feigned confrontation. There were world wars between the different areas of the tiny conurbation, which disobeyed the logic of urban planning. Beira was disobedient from its outset: I was even born and grew up in zones that had been destined for Asians. And football games were held in which the various mixtures defied the racial boundaries of the time. Esturro was, at that stage, my area, my tribe, my nation. Preparations were in hand for the big derby match between Esturro and Ponta-Gea. Our fate was in our hands, or rather in our feet. Joe Hotshot decided to try out his talent as a psychologist on me.

That afternoon, the day before the game, Hotshot called me over. He wore a solemn, serious expression. He made me sit on the wall in front of my house, while he held a long stick in his hand like a huge pencil.

"See the six-yard box here?" he asked, making some scratches in the sand.

The scratches became more complicated as he talked, illustrating my chaotic movement around the pitch. Then, he once again retraced the square of the box:

"Pretend the six-yard box is a girl. That's right, a girl, a chick. You need to open her out, caress her, kiss her. But afterwards . . . afterwards . . ."

"Yes, afterwards?" I asked, half asleep from all the scratching in the sand.

Afterwards. . . Afterwards, I ask: afterwards, at the decisive moment, what must I do?

The allusion made by Joe, the finest coach of all time, was obvious, yet the metaphor eluded me. Love doesn't have an "afterwards." Love is all time, spent in an instant. And I thought of the girls who, during my fifteen years of existence, jostled at the door of my platonic dreams. And I saw Alda, Guida, Isabel, Martinha, Leila, Paula, Mónica, and more than any of the others, Laura, the most recent. And suddenly, it occurred to me: "In matters of love, I only dribble. I don't shoot." This was what suddenly dawned on me.

Joe Hotshot didn't notice my glazed look, lost in other championship contests. And he continued with his carefully drawn-up tactics: the chip shot in direct free kicks, the looping centre in corner kicks, the penalty humdinger. If I lived my football through poetry, Hotshot was a master of prose. His was a language that cleared the pitch of weeds: bicycle kicks, sliding tackles, butterfinger goalies, beating your marker, being up for it, the ball in open play. But I wasn't paying attention. Deep within me, all I could hear was the conflict between myself and my age.

The following day, sporting the colours of the most famous team in the universe, I cast my eyes over the spectators from the middle of the stadium. I can now imagine, many years later, how Cristiano Ronaldo feels when he hears the crowd's engulfing clamour. In my local stadium, the crowd was the whole of humanity. I mainly noticed the girls in the front row, squeezed together so as not to miss a single moment of the game. Suddenly, reality overcame my daydreaming and I looked more closely at the spectators: there they were, the girls. Real, up for the fight in body and soul. There they were, unmistakable in their physique, distracting me in my movements. And in particular, there was Laura, the most beautiful of them all. My instinctive wisdom caused me to turn my gaze towards the coach. Hotshot's mischievous grin confirmed everything: it was a plan schemed up by him. In the face of the object of my passion, there was nothing for it but for me to score goals. Without goals, no one wins. Yet again, I didn't score in that game. And much to the sadness of our coach, we didn't win. I don't know why I say "we." For in the end, I won. It wasn't in the game. Nor in the moments that followed. It was later, when everything assumed the taste of the irreversible. You'll understand in a minute.

The next day, I got a visit from Laura. Her voice was so full of voices that for many years, I remembered her through that abstract presence. And she asked me:

"Are you sad because of the game?"

"I'm sad because of me."

Laura was older, she knew of things that I only suspected. She unfolded a piece of paper scrawled on in her own handwriting.

"It's a poem," she whispered.

"Is it for me?" I asked.

And she answered: "No, it's for Ademir." The other's name hit me like a blow from a catapult, as if I'd suddenly been dropped as a striker, banned from playing. I put the paper in my pocket and screwed it up angrily. More than our defeat, it was Laura's interest in someone else that hurt me. And off I went into my solitude. Laura even phoned a few times. I refused to take the call. In due course, she stopped trying.

I never read the poem. I met Laura again years later, when she already bore the burden of being the mother of someone's mother. I didn't recognize her. Only her tinkling stream of a voice brought me back to its source. It was she who reminded me how she had tried to get in touch again after her last visit. I asked after Ademir. "Who's Ademir?" she asked, puzzled. "I've never met anyone by that name." Her reply sounded convincing, so much so that I changed the subject to other gaps and lapses in our memories. When I got home, I looked around for the old bit of paper, which was still there, all screwed up. Laura had even written down the author's name. It was a poem by João Cabral de Melo Neto, and its title was: "Ademir da Guia." And it went like this:

Ademir imposes his game/ a rhythm (and weight) of lead,/a slug, a film in slow motion,/a man in a nightmare.//His liquid rhythm infiltrates/his opponent, thickly, from within/imposes on him what he wishes,//controlling him, putrefying him/A warm rhythm, like a walk through sand,/through the brackish water of a lagoon,/ sapping and then shackling/the most restless opponents.

Shackled to myself, that's what I was after solving the mystery of Laura's little piece of paper. So Ademir wasn't "another." Reflecting upon it, Ademir was me, stuck in the six-yard box, which is the moment of greatest happiness.

I put the old bit of paper away, and overcame a sad smile. Once again, I'd been nutmegged by some poetry. One can be coached in the skills of football. But the only coach for the challenges of life is ourselves.

Article published in *Índico*, the in-flight magazine of Mozambican Airlines (LAM), May 2010.

THE WATERS
OF BIODIVERSITY

BIODIVERSITY? The translator hesitated. His strained expression translated the effort he was making to find an equivalent for "biodiversity" in Xironga. He translated it by elephants. Then, he corrected himself: animals. Seated on the ground, the country folk couldn't conceal their doubts. Whether it was elephants or all animals, the matter required more substantial explanation. And what about people? The translator saw a way out and shot back an answer: yes, people, animals, the land, all together. And he reinforced his words with a sweeping, encircling gesture.

This was the message we were bringing the people of Machangulo. The place is near Maputo, not more than fifty kilometres away. But life there isn't just remote from the capital. It goes on in another world. This other world. Right there on the flank of the great city of Maputo, is one of the most underdeveloped regions of the country. There are few roads, very few schools, and almost no health clinics. In the complete absence of transport, the country folk travel vast distances on foot. The centre of gravity of their lives is not the capital in fact. It's not even inside Mozambique. They look to the South, to South Africa, to Kwazulu-Natal. It's there that they sell produce, and it's there that they go to find work. It's from there that their ancestors came during the Nguni migrations. Many of them speak Zulu, few speak Portuguese.

The meeting I was engaged in was part of a long project to elaborate a management plan for the district of Matutuíne, the southernmost coastal district of Mozambique. Down there, in the far south of the country, the headlands of Pontas de Ouro, Mamoli, and Malongane shimmer in the distance. Beyond these, nothing else shimmers. Or, if it does, it shimmers in some other hidden dimension. And so there we were, biologists and others, trying to put down on paper the infinite complexity of their daily lives. Our biggest challenge was to find, in biodiversity, reasons to embark on programs to generate wealth, and build bridges with modernity. This was to be done in such a way that biodiversity became a seed, instead of a concept; in the end, it was hoped that development would germinate from this.

The specialists, who had come from Maputo, looked at their schedule with an anguished consciousness of time. The experts, as they like to be called, are always in a hurry. As for me, I took delight in the gaps between work. Sitting on the shore of one of the many lagoons, on one of those leisurely afternoons, I didn't notice evening falling. I sat there as if in rapture at the extraordinary beauty of the place. The dunes, covered in an intense green, resembled a motionless sea. The bottom of the hollows cushioned the slumbering lagoons with different colours. Van Gogh would be busier here than I. And he would be more productive. It's here, in Matutuíne, that one of the richest regions of Mozambique can be found: rich in the diversity of its species and blessed with scenery that flirts with the sea, its mirror.

On that afternoon, I let myself cradle myself in the sluggish sensation of a world being born, as if from behind those dunes, gods were still emerging to create the universe. Is it possible the gods might display the haste and pompous air of the advisers from the capital? My situation might not, after all, be so far removed from that of the gods. For the local inhabitants, that lagoon was sacred. Fishing was prohibited there. On its shores, every February, *ucanhu,* the fermented drink with which they celebrated the harvest, was drunk.

The metallic sound of saucepans clashing together awoke me. What was happening? Women and men seemed determined to undo the tranquillity, which is precisely what they did: they were making noise to scare away the hippos. I caught sight of them, indolently waiting in the long grass, weighing the risks of venturing out into the fields where the villagers tended their crops. One of the men came over to me. He was carrying dried palm leaves with which he lit small fires. Saucepans and flames combined together in the task of chasing away these thick-skinned mammals. The man took the opportunity to accuse me:

"See? And you people come here to protect animals . . ."

I didn't answer. There would be little point in arguing. There would be little use in saying that animals and people can reach ways of living together and even benefiting each other. The countryman would listen with his usual good manners and timeless patience. But deep inside, he would remain fixed in his own sense of righteousness. What we need are examples, practical models that prove how our ideas work. And these models require time. The advisers don't have time.

The following morning, I awoke with the sun. From the high point where I had put up my tent, one could see water on both sides. Towards the interior, there were the still waters of Maputo Bay, with the island of Inhaca and the wide estuary of the Maputo River. In the opposite direction was the limitless Indian Ocean, with its deeper blue. I made my way to the building where our meeting was being held, when someone informed me that the biodiversity had passed that way in the early morning. "Biodiversity?" I asked. There was laughter by way of a reply. It had been the elephants, a huge herd that had survived the war and poachers. They've been there forever, renewing the Futi Corridor that provides their link to neighbouring South Africa. One of the intentions of the Mozambican and South African governments is to protect this ancient route and turn it into one of the focal points for cross-border conservation. The fact that there is nothing in the region is, without doubt, a negative, but it can be turned into the opposite. The low population density, the existence of pristine dune forests of unique vegetation, and the potential for fauna, are all reasons to believe in the future of this place. Some years ago, an internationally known South African scientist, A.E. van Wyk, visited and studied this same region. The South Africans call the area Maputaland. Fascinated by its biological richness, Van Wyk made a proposal that Maputaland should be declared an endemism zone of universal importance. The region's name began to feature in all the literature relating to biodiversity.

The inhabitants of Matutuíne don't know the word. But they know perfectly well what biodiversity is. It's not a conceptual issue. They live on the back of biodiversity. They survive in their little corner, which is so near and yet so remote. We need to create the bridge that will break their historic isolation, but let it be a bridge that both takes and brings in equal measure. And not one of those bridges built to take everything out without giving anything back.

Article published in *Índico*, April 2004.

AS IF THE SEA
HAD ANOTHER SHORE

N O ONE in fact ever travels to an island. Islands exist within us, like a territory we have dreamt of, like a piece of our past that has broken free of time. In me, this insular ghost first appeared when Jonito died and my parents told me he'd gone to an island in the middle of the Chiveve. I was a kid, Jonito was a toad and the Chiveve wasn't even a real river. How could a little stream like that have enough water to contain an island? But in those days, nothing was real. And Jonito spent my whole childhood, crawling, cautious and sluggish, around that little piece of earth surrounded by dark waters.

This is why it now sounds strange to me that I should be entering into an agreement with Mamudo for him to take me out to the islands tomorrow. I use the term "islands" in the plural, but I shall be lucky if the little sailing dhow gets to any island at all.

I have to confess that it wasn't easy to reach an agreement. For negotiations to go well, they shouldn't be easy. At least here, on the coast of Cabo Delgado. The sellers approach as noiselessly as shadows, as if the sand were carpeted to cushion their arrival. In the south of Mozambique, where I come from, they would have accosted me differently:

"I'm selling things."

And the commercial relationship would have been defined immediately, a non-symmetrical relationship between the person with the product and the one with money. The price is within reach. Any thing above that is considered a tip. Not so here. The approach is more professional from the start. The seller announces himself like this:

"I have a deal for you."

And we are both on the same side of the table, knowing in advance that there's going to be a game of verbal give-and-take that will go on for some time. That was how Mamudo approached me. The visit to the "islands" (he kept using the plural) was a complete package. He would provide the boat, he would be the sailor and the steward (serving a meal that he himself would prepare). After agreeing on the price, there was still need for an advance so that he could buy the food. All with the utmost propriety, because as he himself said, everyone in the neighbourhood could vouch for his good name.

The "deal" was completed and a tourist couple who had been listening to the conversation asked whether they could join the expedition. Mamudo then drew up an addendum to the agreement I had already signed.

I went to bed early because our departure the following morning would be at an hour when, according to Mamudo, even the fish would still be sleeping. I dreamt I was some marine creature gliding through those transparent waters, brushing against coral reefs and the dark bellies of dinghies. But in the middle of the night, I was awoken by the noise of a window rattling. A gale was beginning to blow. The fine white sand was being thrown against the wooden walls of my chalet. The beach was gradually invading the floor of my room.

In the morning, it was obvious that the excursion would have to be postponed. When I reached the place at which we were to meet, the tourists were complaining to Mamudo and demanding their money back. But the sailor had already spent the advance the previous day. A second storm was brewing: the tourists' complaints were getting louder. They were going back to Maputo later that day and didn't have time to waste. I decided to intervene, placating the foreigners in their excitement. And it worked: at the end of the morning, under a leaden sky, we all sat on Mamudo's veranda eating the chicken that he had grilled. And there we remained, listening to stories that Mamudo reeled off like the beads on an endless rosary. Each story was a paddle cutting through waters that took us further and further away from the world. At the end, the sailor brought us a basin of warm water to wash our hands. And he said:

"Life is a deal."

Not a particularly poetic image, but that was his way of romanticizing the miraculous way we had celebrated our encounter. When the tourists took their leave, there was a smile on their faces as if they had, after all, visited an island and its paradise. In the end, the sailor kept his promise: without leaving the beach, he had taken us on a journey to the sea's far shore.

Article published in *Índico*, July 2009.

THE CHINA
WITHIN US

CHINA was once the smallest country in the world. And the Chinese the smallest human group on the planet. It happened when I was a child. The universe was a back garden in which to play, and all the Chinese fit in just a few streets of my native city. At that time, the Chinese in Beira were not like those today, light-skinned with smooth hair. Many of them were of mixed race, with frizzy hair and brown skin, frequenting the same churches and schools as the Europeans in the colony.

It happened in Maquinino, the district where I was born. I would leave home on my way to the António Enes Primary School and would pass the shop they used to call the "Cantina Chinesa," to buy exercise books, pencils and the recently arrived Bic pens. There I would join my classmate, the shop owner's son. This boy, whose name was Ching, was reserved and serious, like an adult who had nothing left to dream.

For him, childhood was a task to be carried out with professional diligence. Ching's zealous discretion was the sign of a sturdier race. To be Chinese was to be like that, consigned and devoted to silence. Ching knew arithmetic, but he had no answer when asked where China was, or what it was like. He had been born right there in that African district and his world stopped there, between Munhava, Manga and Macuti.

In 1960, there were about two thousand Chinese registered in Mozambique. More than half of these had been born in Mozambican territory and my little colleague, Ching, was one of these descendants of immigrants. Almost all the seven hundred Chinese who lived in Beira had recent or more remote links with Canton, the land of their ancestral origins. The parents spoke Cantonese among themselves, Portuguese with their children, and Chissena with their customers. A soul distributed in this way might have been sowing seeds for the future.

On Sundays, Ching and I sometimes rode our "donkeys" (that's what we called our bicycles) along the banks of the Chiveve, to watch the fishermen catching eels and women selling shad. The little Chinese gazed at the sun going down over the muddy waters and his narrow eyes seemed to catch sight of landscapes on the other side of the ocean. One day, he invited me to go and see a basketball game. His beloved team, Atlético Chinês, were playing.

"My father doesn't let me say the name of the club in Portuguese," he confessed.

"So what other name does the club have?"

"It's the Tung Hua Athletic Club."

As he reeled off those words in one breath, it was as if he suddenly became a stranger to me. But all Ching wanted was for me to witness the matchless skills of a female player who would be playing for the Portuguese national team that same year. Her name was Sui Mei.

"My father doesn't let me call the player by that name," he confessed once again.

"So what do you call her, then?"

"Swi Mai, that's what we're supposed to call her."

Whether she was Sui Mei or Swi Mai, she was an excellent basketball player. But it wasn't her sporting skill that most impressed me. What left a lasting impression was the grace and elegance of her movements around the court, as if the game were a shared dance and not a contest between opposing sides. Sui Mei's affability seemed to be curing our city of an age-old wound.

"Look at her hair," my friend Ching suggested.

"What about it?"

"See how there isn't a single strand out of place."

The crowd was almost shouting the house down. The players pirouetted through the air, but the Chinese girl's smile and hair were as neat as a pin.

One day, one of Ching's cousins arrived in Beira from Inhaminga. He was a mulatto, the son of a black woman and a Chinese soldier who had fled Canton. His father wanted to send him to study in China. His mother "kidnapped" the boy and took him to the area round Inhaminga. The kid grew up there, in that remote shadow, far from his austere father. His body had grown bigger, as had his anxiety to know his origins. He had now come to the city in order to catch a secret glimpse of his progenitor. We took him to the market and Ching pointed ahead through the crowd.

"There, that's your father!"

The lad stood impassively, and a vague look lingered on his face, as if that vision had no place to dwell within him. I tried to scrutinize the visitor's state of mind: there was a great wall hiding his intimate thoughts.

As we returned, we sensed a deep sadness in him. Ching's enthusiastic invitation took me by surprise:

"How about going to watch the basketball? Sui Mei's playing today, come on, let's go!"

As we sat on the stone bench in the sports pavilion, and listened to the rhythm of the ball as if it were the beating of a heart, the cousin's sad expression lightened, and he even smiled.

It might have been a forced smile, but it was still a smile.

The Olympic Games, Magical Games

Forty years later, in the sitting room of my house, the family clusters round the television, as if it were some luminous oracle.

"Look: they're showing images of Peking!"

"It's not Peking, it's Beijing," someone corrects.

Whether it's Peking or Beijing, it's an almost religious moment. The opening ceremony of the Beijing Olympic Games brings with it a moment of rapture that transports us back to childhood. How long ago it seems since China was a small nation and the Chinese fit into a small area of a small city! China had, after all, always been enormous, a power throughout its history. However, this celebration seems to have been made for me to travel into my own memories. In the spectacle, China travels beyond History, beyond itself. And it's no longer the ceremony I'm watching. It's memories that come alive within me.

Suddenly, I recall little Ching's sad figure, walking along the paths of Maquinino with a missionary's step. The little boy comes from far away, from that time when the Sino-Africans were treated as second-class citizens and learned to be ashamed of their religious and cultural origin.

And now, when the Mozambican flag can be seen in the Olympic Stadium, I recall the boy who came from Inhaminga to heal his feeling of orphanhood. No one is now separated from their family: the message conveyed by the Olympic celebration is a handkerchief waving away the sadness in the faces of all small boys far removed from their childhoods.

Finally, the image of Lurdes Mutola lights up the screen as if her face were already a confirmation of victory. And we noisily rejoice as we watch, as if there were other Olympics within that great festivity.

Gradually, the ever-smiling Sui Mei is born again within me, the girl who healed the wounds of our vanquished lives. And once again, we are all natives of that land where gunpowder was invented to make fireworks sparkle.

Article published in *Índico*, October 2008.

THE CITY ON THE
VERANDA OF TIME

LIKE ALL CITIES, Maputo was fashioned out of invention and myth. The city of red acacias: the first invention. Acacias aren't really acacias. Second fallacy: the splendid trees that embellish the city originate in the continent of Africa. They came from Madagascar. What does their origin matter if they were installed, in all their colour and perfume, in the cityscape of the Mozambican capital? They are just like its inhabitants, most of whom nowadays come from other regions. Third misunderstanding: the name. After Independence, an indigenous name was chosen so as to help return the city to the country that was in the process of being born. Lourenço Marques was brought down from its pedestal and Maputo raised as if evoking a dream. However, the new name did not appear to satisfy the demands of historical and geographical rigour. Maputo is a watery name, the name of the river that flows out into the southern part of the bay. There are those who say that it would be more correct to call it Pfumo or KaMpfumo.

Incontrovertible truths are details that survive the passage of time. For example, take those streets that are carpeted with jacaranda flowers. There, next to the Hospital, who has the courage to step on that lilac-coloured ground? This city, which switched its name from Lourenço Marques to Maputo, is still called Xilunguine by many of its inhabitants. Xilunguine is the place where whites live. Indeed, the city is the door through which the country conducts its barter with modernity. This is the veranda where the world woos the Mozambican nation most persistently. Mozambicanness transits through here, and it is here that our multicultural identity, which is our very claim to citizenship, is woven and interwoven.

The city has been criss-crossed by time and by different worlds. The colonial past lives on in many, often beautiful buildings. The revolutionary period is still present, with its now-faded words staining walls and façades. A slogan fades with time, grows old. If it wasn't born already old. The old houses in the upper part of the city—especially those next to the Polana district—bear witness to an early period, when the Barreira Vermelha area was first settled and the city assumed the pompous sobriquet of "the new Buenos Aires."

This was at the turn of the century and the city's inhabitants were seeking refuge from the low-lying areas, which were marshy and unhealthy. Until the end of the nineteenth century, Lourenço Marques never succeeded in breaking out of the cane palisade extending along a sandy bank, which now houses FACIM (the Maputo Agro-Commercial and Industrial Fair). Everything was contained within this narrow strip, where the Portuguese felt safer. Up above, on the higher ground, was the bush, and to the north, the muddy territories of the mangrove swamps.

A stroll through modern Maputo allows us to read these signs of History. The city is recent but, as in a shell, the different ages became juxtaposed in layers. Another logic then organized the urban space on grounds of race, class, civilization. What was sought was the mirror of a certain type of Europe, as if it were the Mediterranean, rather than the Indian

Ocean lying next to it. Later, the city was disarranged and rearranged, sometimes in the naïve hope of accommodating everyone and allowing itself to be inhabited in a spirit of equality. Under attack from the countryside, the city resists. Managed by the demands of urgency and the ever-insufficient funds, Maputo's beauty eventually imposes itself even after the most difficult moments such as last February's heavy rains.

Some trees resist as well. Some of them are monuments. The old *phama* in Xipamanine that gave its name to the area. The *kigelia* in front of the fort: how many stories, how many myths? It's worth visiting African cities for their trees, which contain legends, and are laden with more stories than foliage.

A Place Where Hybridities Are Made

Much is known about Maputo's historic and architectural heritage. But the city has other lesser-known merits. Maputo was the melting pot for experimentation in new artistic currents. It was there that much of Mozambique's art and thought were forged.

Over a period of decades, the suburbs of old Lourenço Marques had the atmosphere of a borderland, a place of cultural hybridity. In districts like Mafalala, Malanga, Xipamanine and even Malhangalene, space was no longer ordered completely along the lines of race.

It was in areas like these that the cultural hybridity that is the basis of Mozambican thought was forged. In these borderland areas, exchanges were woven not only between races but between cultures. The importance of Makua communities in districts like Mafalala is well known. From a cultural point of view, these areas were highly productive.

During the second half of last century, this suburban belt constituted a series of extremely active cultural niches. Names such as Noémia de Sousa, José Craveirinha, Chichorro, Malangatana, Calane da Silva, the guitar player Daíco, the musical group Djambo, are all products of this cultural conviviality. However, it wasn't only art but actual political thought that germinated in these peripheral areas—civic centres (the African Association), newspapers such as the *Brado Africano*, student associations (NESAMO, the Nucleus for Mozambican African Secondary School Students), all this agitation occurred on the urban periphery as if a new world were being born from the outside, an invasion from the skin that aims towards the centre.

It is quite common for suburban districts like these, inhabited by the working classes, to be the limbo where artistic currents are renewed. Samba first emerged in the suburbs of Rio de Janeiro, tango was born in the suburbs of Buenos Aires. We can, without doubt, detect a similar tendency in the suburbs of Maputo—Fany Mpfumo and Marrabenta music, José Craveirinha and the new poetry, Malangatana with his hugely innovative impulse in painting, Alberto Chissano in sculpture. And we could add Chichorro, the painter of women waiting for marriage on their verandas. Maputo continues, like Chichorro's women: biding time on its wide veranda that looks out over and into itself.

Article published in *Índico*, July 2000.

MOZAMBIQUE:
TWENTY-FIVE YEARS

O N INDEPENDENCE DAY, I was 19. As an adolescent the dream of one day seeing a flag raised for my country had grown gradually stronger. At the time, I believed that a dream could be expressed through a flag. There are things we do because we believe in them. Other things we begin to do because we have ceased to believe. But in 1975, I was a journalist motivated by belief. The world was my church, men my religion. And everything was still possible.

My memory isn't good, but I remember this very clearly. On the night of 25th June, I was scheduled to be on duty at the headquarters of the National Radio Station. For me, it was a punishment to be isolated from the great festivities that were taking place in the Machava Stadium. But we were asked to show discipline and we had to accept that some would have to make sacrifices on behalf of others. It was all part of the belief.

At a quarter to midnight, I and three other journalists decided we were going to be disobedient. There was a rusty old car at the office, and there was someone who thought he could drive. And so we fled the newsroom and off we went in the direction of the stadium, like insects attracted by the seductiveness of light. On the way, I savoured the vague thrill of having transgressed and of joining the collective celebration.

Although there was no traffic, our old car crept along slowly. "At this speed, we'll never get there in time," someone commented. At this point, we suddenly heard sirens, and in an instant, we found ourselves caught in an endless line of cars. To our indescribable shock, President Samora Machel was travelling in one of the vehicles. It was the presidential motorcade that was heading for the ceremony and was slightly late. By some happy accident, our old jalopy ended up being absorbed into the motorcade. So that was how, infiltrating ourselves among high-ranking figures, we entered the stadium, thronged by the clamouring crowds.

I shall never forget those glowing faces, spellbound and enraptured; I shall never forget the look of those who were building that moment. There was rejoicing, the celebration of our being people, of having our land and deserving the heavens. More than a country, we were celebrating another destiny for our lives. It was a kind of redemption, a re-encounter with our own future.

Twenty-five years later does the average Mozambican wear the same expression? No. Nor could that ever be. For during the first of those twenty-five years, a total, absolute hope took shape. It was a legitimate, but naïve hope that it would be possible, within a generation, to change the world and redistribute happiness. Between the optimism of demagogy and pessimist defeatism, what balance can be drawn up for this period? These have been, above all, years of learning what sovereignty and dignity are, and what they can be. As a nation, we haven't learned to walk yet, while we share the same dreams and disillusions. We would no longer rush to a stadium with the same childlike joy to celebrate a new annunciation. But that doesn't mean we are any less disposed to have beliefs. We shall be more alert to the knowledge that everything needs a direction and a time. We feel the pulse of a world that simultaneously requests us to show citizenship while also denying us it.

A quarter of a century is a long time in the history of an individual. But it's almost nothing in the history of a country. Today, we know that we are still a long way from fulfilling the dream that caused us to sing and dance in the Machava Stadium on the 25th of June. Most of our aspirations are still to be achieved. We can resort to explanations, point the finger of blame, but none of this will be very productive. We shall need to invent within us reasons to act. With greater or lesser belief, but in a process of construction. Not the best of all futures, but a future for everyone: a future that may begin this very day. Mozambique is no more than this process of construction, this commitment to our children.

Article published in *Índico*, October 2000.

A SEA OF EXCHANGE,
AN OCEAN OF MYTHS

THE INDIAN OCEAN isn't just a geographical landmark: it is the guardian of the history of diverse peoples. Voyages of old didn't just exchange genes, merchandise, languages and cultures. Identities were forged as well as a common history for peoples who could nowadays well be termed "Indianic."

Adepts of genetic and/or cultural "purity," don't delude yourselves: our identities today are the results of ancient hybridities, so old and complex that we can't always trace them. This mixture of mixtures is, of course, common to all humanity. Around the Indian Ocean, however, where a dense web of exchanges began seven centuries ago, this mosaic is absolutely unique.

The coast of Mozambique bears witness to these navigators. In specific localities specific memories are preserved: the departure of slaves, the presence of traders, the establishment of a military presence. To these territories endless processions of ships and sailors arrived. Chinese, Indonesians, Arabs, Indians, Europeans all passed through here. It was through the coast of Mozambique that the coconut palm and the banana tree penetrated the entire continent, bringing change to the lives of whole communities. It was through these exchanges that the Indian Ocean bathed remote lands which its waters never touched. More than bringing products, the visitors from distant places left an ability to establish trading relationships and negotiate conditions. And it wasn't just clothes, ships, seeds and fruits that the "others" brought (items which we nowadays simplistically believe to be ours in origin). What we were left with was a capacity for cultural hybridity, to create identities for ourselves that function like import-export enterprises. it was also an undoing of identity that we ceded to others who, in this way, gradually became less other.

Other Globalizations

The sailor who helped Vasco da Gama navigate from Mozambique Island to India wasn't aware of the extent to which he was participating in what we now call "globalization." Nor did he have any idea how much he was repeating an act that had already been carried out almost a century before.

In fact, in 1403, the Chinese admiral Zheng He commanded a fleet of ships that called in along the East African coast. He was sailing in the opposite direction to the Portuguese, but he too was helped by a Muslim sailor who was familiar with the routes of the Indian Ocean. Zheng He himself converted to Islam and occasionally went to Mecca to fulfil his spiritual obligations. The seas were becoming highways for men and for gods.

Between 1403 and 1435, Admiral Zheng He crossed the Indian Ocean seven times. During this period, a total of 350 great junks sent by the Ming emperor transported people and goods between the different regions that bordered on the Indian Ocean.

The Chinese junks weren't small ships. Some of them rivalled modern ocean liners in size. They could carry a thousand passengers and hundreds of tons of merchandise. They sailed aided by currents and monsoons that blew sails fastened to bamboo spars. Unlike Portuguese ships, which had three masts, the Chinese ships were equipped with nine. Neither Vasco da Gama at the end of the century nor Zheng He at the beginning inaugurated new routes across the waters of the Indian Ocean. Both of them followed routes already pioneered by Islam and by Arab traders.

Unlike the South Atlantic, which, in the fifteenth century, had not yet witnessed intercontinental voyages, the waters of the Indian Ocean had already seen many a ship. The islands that the Portuguese discovered along their route were uninhabited. The same was not true of Africa's east coast.

Other Passengers

It is difficult for us to imagine how much trade took place in the 14th century between such distant places. We assume that such difficult journeys require modern, sophisticated nautical instruments. But the challenge of crossing oceans has long stimulated the art and ingenuity of human beings. We never accept our destiny and to the place allotted to us. We have always shared the miracle of journeying across waters with the gods.

The ships also brought mistakes and misunderstandings. When Columbus disembarked on the American coast, he baptized the local inhabitants "Indians." He believed that he was encountering people of the Indies, in the Indian Ocean. The name, the fruit of an error, was never rectified. The name stuck forever and for everyone (including the barely baptized "Indians"). Other influences survived for centuries. The ships didn't only bring riches but furtive stowaways known as rats. The rats were notable spreaders of disease and plague. The history of these voyages is not one consisting only of courage. European navigators brought with them ill-nesses against which the inhabitants of the Americas had not acquired any resistance. Epidemics killed millions of these "Indians." It is believed that within a century of the arrival of Columbus, some of these peoples had been reduced to one-tenth of their original population.

The voyages generated trade in foodstuffs. Much of what we incorporate in our daily diet comes from the Americas. The Portuguese navigators were largely responsible for this dis-semination. Many Mozambicans believe that products such as manioc, sweet potato, cashews, peanuts, guavas and papayas are genuinely African. They were all imported and arrived in Africa in the hold of some little Portuguese sailing ship.

A Cloth of Many Threads

Rather than an obstacle, the Indian Ocean was a route, a cultural crossroads. Navigators from other continents, other races, and other religions, arrived over its waters. On the coast of Mozambique, the ships were the needle that stitched together this huge cloth, which even today is covered with an immense number and variety of different prints. For centuries, it wasn't just trade in goods, languages and cultures that took place. Nations were built. Mozambique was woven together from the coast towards the interior. The thread that gathers our country came from water, from travel, from the desire to be others. The flag that covers us is a cloth of many, diverse threads.

Article published in *Índico*, January 2000.

THE SWEET
TASTE OF SURA

T HE DHOW crosses the waters, undulating over a liquid
mirror. The little boat is a narcissist. Arab in its origin,
the sailing craft contemplates itself with the slowness
of a time that no longer exists. It's the Bay of Inhambane, and
its vocation is that of all bays: its waters rue not being the open
sea, allowing themselves to lull in the earth's embrace. This
curved bight is crossed by the fishermen, traders and travellers who link Inhambane and Maxixe. People who still have
the same feeling for time as that which witnessed the place's
creation. One of the most beautiful places in Mozambique.

Geologists, who know how to read landscapes, look at the
bay's configuration somewhat skeptically. At some far-off time,
the Bay of Inhambane may have been something else: for
example, a closed lagoon, like the ones at Quissico or Poelela.
The lagoon got tired of existing all by itself, so it opened one
arm to the east. Nowadays, dhows comb the placid waters of
the bay, but they know they have to obey the intricate design of
the channels. Some of these underwater valleys are deep and
reach depths of twenty metres.

Coconut trees and mangroves line the coastal entrance.
It's like a green frame enclosing blue. The southern limit of the

bay is formed by a huge peninsula supported by dunes that undulate like a gigantic dhow imitating the sea. The highest dunes, such as Condjane that has a height of sixty metres, are interspersed with low-lying terrain where rainwater accumulates. Over these dunes, forests still survive, and some of them are considered sacred terrain, where the original founders of the place repose. The lagoons below attract flocks of birds, among them the famous "hammerhead" about which legends of witchcraft persist. In nearby trees, one can find the no-less-famous nest of this bird. Unlucky is the person who, even unwittingly, destroys one of these huge, clumsy nests. The punishment is everlasting madness.

The Bay of Inhambane provides shelter for dolphins, whales and giant turtles. The rare and almost extinct-mammal, the dugong, can be found in the inlet at Linga-Linga. It is generally believed that one of the largest populations of this mammal on the whole of Mozambique's coast survives here. There are also terrestrial mammals such as the rare, furtive, mongoose (*vungué* in the local language). There are small bush babies (*bwanga*) and black-faced monkeys (*nzoko*).

An extensive mangrove swamp rings much of the bay. This marshy forest is crossed by deep channels that are used for fishing. In one of the tourist establishments here, they had the happy idea of building a boardwalk into the mangrove. Tourists can venture along this pleasant pathway and discover the incomparable beauty of this ecosystem. At low tide, millions of tiny crabs carpet the ground, creating the impression that the sands are boiling.

A World of Interweavings

The best thing about Inhambane Bay, however, is the people: their inexhaustible hospitality and their infinite willingness to share their time and their soul with you. On one of the many occasions when I have worked in that region as a biologist, I made friends with someone who left a deep impression on me. It was an old fisherman who showed me the way to a place where flamingos arrived, and he gave me, without knowing it, the title of one of my novels. I met Afonso Nhalane in one of those mangrove channels that are flooded at high tide. He had just finished checking his gillnet for trapping fish. He shook his head: the fish he'd caught would only provide one meal. Nothing more. Dragging his feet, as if he was the one who'd been trapped in some invisible net, the man climbed the dune and sat down in the shade of a palm tree.

Nhalane's destiny is linked to palm trees. One can see immediately from his name: Nhala is the name of one of those palms from which *sura* is extracted. Afonso Nhalane recalls that in the olden days, there were more fish, more flamingos. Is this nostalgia for his youth, that time when, according to him, there was more of everything? But the fisherman insists: fishing with gillnets, selling *sura* (the famous palm wine), selling coconuts, all that was enough. Now, life is like the bay begging for ever more streams. But he doesn't complain, and is resigned to selling the few chickens he breeds in his large backyard. "What am I now," he asks, "a chicken fisherman? That's what I am," he repeats, "a fisherman of chicken."

He invites me to go and have a glass of *sura* at his house. The sale of this beverage was once an important part of the family's budget. Now, it's only used to welcome visitors like myself. On the way there, we cross his landholding. He knows each of his coconut palms. He almost seems to greet them, calling each one by its name.

Later, with a glass of *sura* already half drunk, we sit catching the breeze that comes off the sea in the afternoon. We are leaning against a palisade made of plaited coconut leaves. The fisherman notes my fascination at the intricacy of the interwoven patterns of the palisade.

"Nowhere else will you find these plaits. Only here in Inhambane."

The word fills me like the breeze: "plaits." That's what the fisherman and I are doing with the time: plaiting away the hours, between conversation and the excuse for another glass. As I take my leave, I pass groups of girls plaiting each other's hair in turn. And I walk away towards the sun as it plaits away the afternoon in the background.

Article published in *Índico*, October 2003.

LAND OF
WATER AND RAIN

O NE of my brothers, when he was a child and in a bad
mood, would threaten:
"I'm going to run away to Inhaminga."
What he was trying to say was that he was going beyond
the world, to where there were no more roads. He was going
beyond the limit from which it was possible to return, and
by doing this, he was putting our love for him to the test. It
was a game without any risk: our love was greater than any
distance.

Inhaminga was situated in some inaccessible fog. It was the
farthest place that we, who were born and lived in Beira, could
imagine. At the time, the district of Inhaminga, in the province of Sofala, was really remote. Not just because of the time
we took to get there, but because of the variety of scenery, and
the extraordinary worlds that we passed on our journey. There
were still abundant woodlands of miombo trees, crossed by
thousands of streams that swelled up with the slightest rain.
Lions, buffalo, leopards, the inhabitants of a mystical world,
all wandered through the area. To survive, people there said
one needed to eat snakes and kill wild and ferocious animals. Forty years later, I make a return journey through this

bewitching region. The first impression that strikes us on these incursions into the past is that the world has shrunk. What I remembered as great highways of sand were, after all, what they had always been: narrow tracks. A child's eyes make the world gigantic. And I am at a loss before my second confrontation with the past: the forest has been pushed out of the landscape. There are still a few patches in the areas that are most difficult to reach. Nor could it be otherwise: these tracks which, after all, cross the savannah were opened up by loggers and the owners of sawmills. It was they who, for more than fifty years, had carved out these roads for their trucks. With the loggers came the hunters. And farmers grew in numbers, forcing the trees to retreat forever.

To the northwest, the famous Gorongosa Park is still a refuge for this canopy of greenery and mystery.

As I went on, I began to feel some unease in my heart. The road between Dondo and Inhaminga is easy to negotiate during the dry season. My car, however, would stop at the slightest excuse. The shacks along the side of the road, the country villages, the charcoal burners' encampments, the level crossings along the newly reconstructed Sena railway line, all were a reason for me to jump out of my car and get talking to the people of the area. In the beginning, I was able to remember the local language, Chissena, only vaguely. But almost all of them spoke Portuguese. Like those fishermen who use a harpoon with a sharp point to comb through the deep mud of dried-up lagoons. Somewhere there is a tasty fish that lies buried during the dry season, awaiting the arrival of the rains. Further away, the storks with their wax bills compete with the fishermen. Their technique is, after all, similar: to take the distracted fish by surprise, and spear it.

I drive among hundreds of bicycles loaded with bags of charcoal and women carrying fish traps on their heads. The area is very poor, possibly among the poorest in Sofala. The trade in fish, charcoal and homemade beverages is what allows them to eke out a living. Yet there is a joviality in their behaviour, as if the future of the world were within their grasp and hope were at hand. I forget my initial sensation that something had been lost between my memory and the present.

Evaristo Faife is the region's headman. It is he who reopens doors to a world that doesn't require sophistry. Next to him are two countrymen, Sindique and Valicho. They have all experienced various wars, and have no wish to recall those turbulent times. The men agree to show me around and to help me in my work of recording the fauna that survives along the banks of the Sangussi River.

Next day, I meet a group of South African tourists who are there for birdwatching. That is how they introduce themselves, as if they were proudly claiming some rare ethnic identity. They are accommodated in tents, with few comforts, but in total harmony with the local inhabitants. They are on the lookout for rare and endemic birds such as the palm-nut vulture, the blue quail, and the green-headed oriole. I'm not too surprised to encounter such a group. The area to the north of Dondo is, in fact, an important international focal point for birdwatchers. The birdlife found there is famous for its rarity and for the number of species that are endemic to the area. They invite me to have dinner with them, and we share some tinned food accompanying a rice concoction they have all had a hand in making. They are happy because, that afternoon, they have been watching groups of wattled broadbills, a protected bird that can only be found in flood-prone grasslands, the *tandos*.

We fall asleep to the gentle but monotonous croaking of the frogs. These musical reptiles remind us that the surrounding area is a region where land and water vie with each other. Between the great Savane and Sangussi rivers, there are dozens of small water courses that flow from the grasslands towards the sea. Not far away, other tourists enjoy the Savane beach, to the north of the city of Beira.

At night, I tell the headman the story about my brother, and his use of Inhaminga as a means of emotional blackmail. The man laughs. Then a certain melancholy invades Evaristo Faife's face, and he says:

"Your brother was right: this place is more remote than abroad."

"That's not true. Aren't we all together now?"

"Yes, but how long did it take you to come back here?"

I am silent. A nightjar sings nearby. I don't want to give an answer about the length of time between my visits. In that peaceful atmosphere, the only thing I feel like doing is making time slow down.

Article published in *Índico*, July 2004.

FLYING PLACES

THE PLANE seems to hesitate, surrendering to the landscape down below that lazily reveals itself to us as we
gaze at it from our position as temporary birds. It is
not flying over places that marks our memory. It is the extent
to which those places will continue flying within us.

Here's Luanda, the Angolan next to me murmurs. He
speaks with the excitement of someone making a first discovery. For me, it's not the first time. But it is the first time I have sat
on a flight next to an Angolan who has just visited Maputo and
has admitted that the capital of Mozambique left him at a loss
for words.

My friend and travelling companion confessed that
while he found it difficult to accept, Mozambican cities
were inspiring. Now, as we fly over his hometown, he finds
reasons to avoid comparisons. They aren't fabricated reasons:
the war, the refugees, the galloping urban expansion that
swallows the city and steals its civic symmetry. All this has
turned Luanda into an unmanageable space which, now that
peace has returned, has to face the challenge of overcoming
its predicament. In the end, Luanda's problems aren't so distinct from those of Maputo. The difference merely lies in the

degree of intensity with which, and the lapse of time since, each country put its respective war behind it.

The city's streets confirm that impression of chaos common to large African cities. The hectic traffic, the thousands of youths who have transformed their bodies into showcases for goods, the intense colours, the mutilated figures who preserve the scars of a time of suffering: these are the brush strokes of an initial portrait. Gradually, however, the city breaks free of this first impression, and we see how old Luanda, what remains of one of the oldest African cities, hasn't yet been swallowed up.

This is a marked difference with Mozambique: our cities that face the Indian Ocean are much more recent. We're not just talking about civic construction. We are talking about internal architecture, an architecture of the soul that, in Angola, forged a Creole elite. A small part of the city was the possession of this Angolan elite even before Independence occurred. This social phenomenon occurred later and more prosaically in Mozambique. I have visited Luanda on a number of occasions over the last thirty years. What I have seen, and still see, is a city that awakens and moves in an unconstrained way. The weight of its long history and its more recent wounds haven't dampened the energy of Luanda's inhabitants and their capacity for resistance.

My last visit left me very surprised, and in a positive way: the problems, some of which were structural, were still there, but dynamic changes were making themselves visibly felt.

"Things are happening here," an Angolan writer told me.

It's true that the modernization occurring here is sometimes carried out to the detriment of that which should be sacrosanct: the cultural and historical heritage, the deepest roots of the place. Whoever has travelled the world knows that this isn't a local phenomenon. It's a kind of absurd price, a deal that has to be negotiated in the face of the greed of those who think of quick profits at all costs.

Late in the afternoon, I stroll alone along the corniche and contemplate the jumble of houses looking out over the bay. It's impossible not to be left with this image in one's memory. And at night, they take me through the turmoil of the "Ilha," the Island of Luanda. I was already familiar with the vitality of its nightlife, and the parties that only finish the next morning. A playful way of overcoming all constraints. We walk in a limbo of effervescence, and feel this area justifies the creativity that forged *semba, kizomba, kuduru*, the way these rhythms proved able to travel and mingle in other distant lands. The same thing happened with local expressions such as *bué, cota,* and *estamos juntos*. All made in Angola.

But there's something of Maputo in all this nocturnal merrymaking, and I love the similarity that occasionally shows its distinctive quality. My travel companion—who is having dinner with me—contemplates the lights on the other side of the bay, and sighs before saying:

"It reminds you of your hometown, doesn't it?"

I nod in agreement, knowing only too well that the question has another meaning. And I smile not so much at my interlocutor, but because I seem to see the lights of Maputo mirrored in the bay of Luanda. After all, my friend and I know that places cannot be compared. Like people, each one of them occurs at one single moment in time, in one single, unrepeatable life.

Article published in *Índico*, July 2008.

A BOAT IN THE SKY
OVER MUNHAVA

AT WEEKENDS, we would visit Munhava. It was right there, only two districts away, but it was as if we were going to another nation. We would cross just two areas, Matacuane and Esturro, but it was a journey across continents. I was in the back seat of the car, and had to crane my neck to see the streets. For most of the journey, I gaze at the canopies of the coconut palms and the herons that balance on their long leaves. Being a child is having a lot of sky overhead. This illusion flashed by through the car window: to be in the sky, the birds didn't even have to take off.

Even today, Munhava has more sky than ground. And in my daydreamed memory, that's how I recall visits to the area, where the city's water tank stretched upwards like a grey giraffe. We would spend Saturday afternoons there and sleep at the Fernandeses' farm. The Goan couple were so happy that we didn't realize they were going mad. My father had been a colleague of Amarildo Fernandes at the railway company, and their friendship had outlasted this shared experience. At the time, I didn't understand how they could playfully exchange secret messages:

"You're not Goan. You're Portuguese."

"Not at all. I'm from this land," Amarildo would reply, passing his hand over the ground. And he would repeat: "I am this land."

The Fernandes property was so vast that it didn't even appear to have a boundary wall. I would fall asleep as soon as darkness fell, lulled by the cicadas that fear silence more than they do death. The drumbeats, coming from the direction of the Munhava marshlands, reminded us that the walls did exist, and that another kind of merriment was kindling on the other side of the road. Nearer, almost inside the room, frogs belched on an empty stomach. And empty was how the world became. Munhava slept weightlessly in my bed.

I would wake up in the morning when the earth was still asleep, covered only by the moisture of the dew. Amarildo Fernandes would walk through the early morning mist, carrying his shoes.

"Here in Munhava, you don't wet your feet so much if you walk barefoot," he said.

And I would glisten like a drop of dew. I was a kid. Who, in those days, paid any attention to someone of my age? But Amarildo made me feel like a person and would dedicate his first words of the day to me. And, within his Portuguese, he spoke another language unknown to me. For instance, he would say: in Munhava, there's so much water that a tree even gets mixed up with its own roots.

Fernandes was right. In Beira, it was always as if it had just stopped raining. For our host, all this water was a blessing. He was the owner of extensive rice fields; rice has more gills than it has roots, and needs more water than a fish. Only my father reminded us, bitterly:

"So much water here and so many folk without water!"

It was Sunday, and it was early. The house was still asleep. Only I and Amarildo Fernandes were enjoying the first rays of sunlight. It was so light on the farm that only when night fell did I know where the inside of the house was. And there was our host, skipping across ant tracks, a finger to his lips telling us to keep quiet:

"We must let Evelina sleep. Poor soul, she's so thin. Don't you think?"

"Thin, Dona Evelina?"

"Yes, she's certainly thin. She's so thin I don't even notice when she's naked."

On these morning jaunts, Amarildo Fernandes would always take me to see the rice fields, where different tones of green undulated as far as the eye could see. But on this occasion, he took me in his old truck over towards the fuel tanks. And there he started to heave rocks that were bigger than I was. I helped as much as I could. Above all, I helped when we got back to the farm, and he started digging holes in the ground to bury the stones.

Amarildo planting stones? That was the first sign of madness. By this time, my father was awake, and questioned him.

"What am I doing? I'm sowing."

He was doing what country folk do with corn: he was planting three seeds together to bring luck.

"God wants everything in pairs," the planter explained.

"Sorry, but why are you planting three stones then?"

"So that a fourth one will be born."

So that's what happened over the whole of that Sunday: the truck coming and going, Fernandes's skinny arms carrying and then depositing the stones. We returned home in silence, scared that we would have to accept the evidence of our friend's mental illness.

"What was all that about, that rushing around with stones?" my mother asked.

"He said he had a dream."

"Amarildo is always dreaming."

"He said he dreamt the river was flooding Munhava. He dreamt the water was invading his farm."

"Amarildo isn't like me," my old man concluded, in defence of his former colleague. The Goan had always had the backbone of a little bird. The slightest burden left him prostrate. The weight of a dream was too much for his old friend.

"What a miserable world this is. A man like Amarildo assailed just like that by a bad dream . . ."

Beira, we know, is the city of the Chiveve. But not everyone knows that *chiveve* means "flood tide." And the tide that flooded Amarildo Fernandes's dream, a week later eventually burst the banks of the Pungwe, the banks of the Chiveve, and the banks of reality. And when, on that last Sunday, we crossed the oceans that divided us from Munhava, we found the farm covered with water. The house had already detached itself from the ground. It was a boat. On the highest ground was Evelina, surrounded by servants and the possessions she had managed to salvage.

"What about Amarildo?"

He'd waded off through the water. Had he drowned? No. He'd forded the vast sea, like a reborn Christ. Evelina didn't seem concerned. There was no need, in her view, for a rescue party. Her husband had gone to visit the submerged rice fields. And he'd gone to weep over his lost crops. He was bound to return once his tears had been shed. In a sense, he never returned. For he came back, emptied of his soul, drained of reason. Amarildo Fernandes's sanity had drowned along with the green rice fields.

A month later, we were the only ones at the dockside, bidding the Fernandeses farewell. The two of them were so thin that I didn't even notice them disappearing into the belly of the ship. They were leaving for Goa, for other rice fields. And as that ship set off across the waters of the Indian Ocean, it looked to me like the last bird plying the sky over Munhava.

Article published in *Índico*, March 2010.

ABOUT THE AUTHOR

Mia Couto was born in Beira, Mozambique in 1955. In the years after his country gained independence from Portugal, he was director of the Mozambican state news agency, and worked as a newspaper editor and journalist. Since the 1980s, he has combined the profession of environmental biologist with that of writer.

Couto is the author of more than 25 books of fiction, essays and poems that have been translated into more than 20 languages. He has won major literary prizes in Mozambique, Zimbabwe, Portugal, Brazil and Italy. African critics chose his novel *Sleepwalking Land* as one of the twelve best African books of the 20th century. His most recent novel in English, *The Tuner of Silences*, was long-listed for the 2015 Dublin IMPAC Award.

In 2013 Couto was awarded the Camões Prize, given to a Portuguese-language writer for his life's work. In 2014 he received the Neustadt International Prize for Literature, sometimes dubbed the "American Nobel." Couto's books have been bestsellers in Africa, Europe and South America.

Mia Couto lives with his family in Maputo, Mozambique, where he works as an environmental consultant.

ABOUT THE TRANSLATOR

David Brookshaw has translated eight other books by Mia Couto, including *The Tuner of Silences, Sleepwalking Land, Under the Frangipani* and *The Last Flight of the Flamingo*. He is Professor Emeritus in Lusophone Studies at the University of Bristol, with special interests in post-colonial literatures and literary translation.